CW01468382

The Changing Landscapes of Dublin

DUBLINCITYinfo.ie

A new website for Dublin, **www.dublincityinfo.ie**, compiled by Pat Liddy and designed and developed by Kaelleon Design Limited, is now available. The website, which will be continually developed, contains the following sections:

History of Dublin

Timewatch

Origin of Street Names

Famous Residents

Historic Sites

Visitor Centres

Useful Links

Online Shop

(Limited signed prints of the illustrations featured in this book may be ordered using the reference number listed for each picture).

Pat Liddy
And The Changing Landscapes of Dublin

Published on the occasion of the author's exhibition,
Pat Liddy and the Changing Landscapes of Dublin,
held in City Hall, 3rd - 14th September 2003.

dublincityinfo.ie

Published 2003 by dublincityinfo.ie
19 Thorndale Crescent, Dublin 5, Ireland.
Tel: +353 1 831 1109. Fax: +353 1 832 9406
E-mail: info@dublincityinfo.ie
Website: www.dublincityinfo.ie

Copyright in the text © 2003 by Pat Liddy
Copyright in the illustrations and photographs © 2003 by Pat Liddy.
The right of Pat Liddy to be identified as the author of this work has been
asserted by him.

Casebound ISBN 0-9545823-0-6

A catalogue record for this book is available from the British Library.

All rights reserved. No part of this book may be reproduced or utilised in any form or by any means,
electronic or mechanical, including photocopying, recording or by any information storage and retrieval
system without prior permission in writing from the publisher. This publication may not be circulated in
any form of binding or cover other than that in which it is published or without similar conditions as
above being imposed on subsequent purchasers.

Design, typesetting, layout and pre-press origination by
Kaelleon Design Ltd. (Web: www.kaelleondesign.ie, Tel: 01 855 2405)
Repro by Techni Graphoplan Ltd.
Scanning by Digiphoto and Master Photo Ltd.
Printed by Oval Printing Company
Bound by Duffy Bookbinders

Publication supported by:

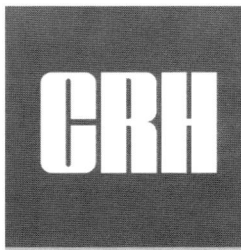

To my Sponsors

I wish to acknowledge, with heartfelt thanks, the support that I received from the following. Their assistance made possible the publication of this book and the holding of my exhibition *Pat Liddy and the Changing Landscapes of Dublin* at City Hall, 3rd - 14th September 2003. In fact without their financial and logistical help neither of these ventures could have taken place.

Sponsor to this Book & Principal Exhibition Sponsor:

CRH

Sponsor to the Exhibition:

Dublin City Council
Comhairle Cathrach Bhaile Átha Cliath

Principal Commissioning Sponsor:

AerRianta

Commissioning Sponsors:

Alcove Properties
C.I.E.
Cyril Carr
Cosgrave Property Group
Dublin Docklands Development Authority
Guinness Ireland Group
Manor Park Homebuilders

National College of Ireland
Railway Procurement Agency
Roches Stores
Sorohan Builders
Stephen's Green Shopping Centre
The Temple Bar
Treasury Holdings

Acknowledgements

I would also like to place on record my thanks to the following individuals for their personal courtesy and help: Jack Golden and Ann Fitzpatrick - *CRH*, Gerry Weir - *Aer Rianta*, Seán Reilly - *Alcove Properties*, Niall Grogan - *C.I.E*, Jim Gahan - *Cosgrave Property Group*, Carmel Smith & Peter Coyne - *Dublin Docklands Development Authority*, Pat Barry - *Guinness Ireland Group*, John Ronan - *Treasury Holdings*, Jackie Cleary - *The Temple Bar*, Dan Boyd - *Stephen's Green Shopping Centre*, Joe Sorohan - *Sorohan Builders*, Patricia Burrell - *Burrell Marketing*, Eamonn Brady - *Railway Procurement Agency*, Diana Roche - *Roches Stores*, Prof. Joyce O'Connor - *National College of Ireland*, John Moran - *Manor Park Homebuilders*, Paul Ferguson - *Map Library, Trinity College*, Tom Kennedy - *Kennedy Publications*, Tom Coffey - *Dublin City Business Association* and Eamonn Elliot - *Ballymun Regeneration*. Much of information available to me for the early years in Dublin's history has come from the dedicated life-long work of Dr Howard Clark - *Department of History* and his colleague Professor Anngret Simms - *Department of Geography, University College Dublin*.

In putting together the exhibition and this book I am especially grateful to: Brian and Callie Scanlon, Bill Maxwell, Anne Marie, Pádraig and Brendan Liddy, Rory McNeela - *The Frame Factory*, John Fitzgerald, Philip Maguire, Kevin Dowling, Jack Gilligan, Doncha Ó Dulaing, Mary Mulcahy, Deirdre Vaughan, Hugh Fahey and Pat McDonnell - *Dublin City Council*, Diane Dixon and Paddy McGrane and the rest of the staff - *City Hall*, Mary Clark - *City Archives*, Joe Beardmore - *Dublin Suburban Rail* and Slava Beskhmelnitskiy.

Finally I cannot forget the unending patience, invaluable advice and technical support I received from: Barry Delves and Gerry Kavanagh - *Master Photo*, Trevor Lee - *Digiphoto*, Conor Arrigan and Marcella Hand - *Kaelleon Design Limited* and John Crimmins and Phil Price - *Oval Printing Company*.

I apologise to anybody whose name I may have inadvertently omitted due to my faulty memory or inadequate note-keeping.

Dedication

Writing books has always been a mixed blessing in our household. My initial enthusiasm for each venture must soon turn to the practicalities of hard work which inevitably corrupts into sheer drudgery, unbelievable pressures and impossible deadlines which can make me almost unliveable with. I am afraid my unflagging optimism never learns from hard experience and so I place yet another tiresome project on my long-suffering family. I again beg their forgiveness, thank them from my heart for their emotional and practical support in so many different ways and promise them that I will never write another book again, ever....at least not until a respectful term has passed. So, Josephine, Anne Marie, Pádraig and Brendan, and my mother, Maureen, who assists with her daily assaults on heaven, take a well deserved bow!

Contents

Courtesy of the National Gallery of Ireland.

Sir Henry Sidney leaving Dublin Castle: *This woodcut from John Derricke's 'Images of Ireland' (1581) depicts the Lord Deputy of Ireland, Sir Henry Sidney, leaving Dublin Castle before commencing a military campaign to subdue the rebellious Irish countryside on behalf of Elizabeth l. It is interesting to note the city's topography from this somewhat romanticised view. There was indeed a moat and twin-towered gateway into Dublin Castle over which are shown here the speared and severed heads of 'traitorous' rebels. The cavalcade is proceeding up Castle Street which is lined with gable-fronted buildings with the tower of Christ Church Cathedral in the background. The collection of buildings and the castle walls in the middle background are a bit misleading as Dublin Castle was not that large. The city walls as such were not that close to the castle at that angle so artistic licence was used in this instance, it would seem. A visitor from that era to the same street now would see absolutely nothing remaining from then. In another four hundred years who can say what will remain of any of our streets from today? One thing is for sure; change is inevitable.*

Introduction

If change is inevitable then it needs to be managed responsibly and sensitively, with thoughtful planning and not without some vision. In this regard Dublin has had a mixed record. Sometimes vision was an end in itself and it rode roughshod over people's rights (as often happened in the much vaunted Georgian period). In more recent times brash development showed scant vision and left unfettered would have wiped away the very character and soul of the city. Some planning decisions in the past were open to corruptive influences or often failed to see the more complex and holistic needs of a living urban environment. Frustrating and hugely expensive delays in decision-making, consultative processes and planning can also be seriously restraining factors in reaching imaginative goals.

Whatever steps are taken in the future, one thing is certain; Dublin is currently seeing change on a scale greater than any historic precedent. The outward spread of the city into the neighbouring counties and beyond has created traffic and travelling nightmares for commuters, public transport and industry. Services and infrastructure simply cannot cope. And this is only the beginning. The population is likely to double to 2 million in the Greater Dublin Area by the year 2030. Yet this increase in numbers may be the very solution for the good health of the city. Infrastructure and adequate public transport will have to be provided for, higher density housing will have to be the norm (this route has already been commenced), inner city living will have to be upgraded to encourage families and older people to take up residency and significant neighbourhood town centres, with every important local facility in place, will have to be developed to help reduce unnecessary car journeys.

This book, based on the author's exhibition held in Dublin's magnificently restored City Hall in September 2003, charts the various eras of Dublin's evolution. A series of pictomaps, paintings and drawings will lead the reader through the centuries of transition, through times of expansion and boom as well as through periods of stagnation and depression. A futuristic look is also taken of what Dublin may look like in the year 2050 which should both tease and fascinate. It will be interesting to revisit this section when 2050 actually comes around and see how different the forecasts will have turned out – hopefully for the better, if that is not being naively optimistic.

Risen by our ancestors
The Standing Stone
Has seen a million changing skies
More fleeting, less steadfast
Will be the pinnacles of today.

Part 01

Mapping the Changes

The earliest known surviving map of Dublin is that drawn by John Speed and dated 1610 (see page 22). This section of the book is an attempt by the author, drawing on archeological, geological and historical research as well as consulting period maps, to reconstruct pictorial-type maps of Dublin from about 1000 AD right up to the present and, conjecturally, beyond to the year 2050. While the author has made every attempt to be as accurate as possible, his emphasis was on the artistic interpretation rather than on cartographical exactitude.

Dublin Bay: This view looks from over the Irish Sea westwards and represents the topographical appearance of the Dublin Bay region and its hinterland after the ending of the last Ice Age around 12,000 years ago. This period was long before the arrival of human habitation which was around c.7000BC. The land reclamations and harbour installations that define present-day Dublin Bay have, of course, yet to make their appearances. The larger rivers such as the Liffey, Dodder, Poddle and Tolka (the only ones shown in the painting) flow into their wide estuaries without hindrance or restriction. The Dublin and Wicklow Hills, then more rugged and forbidding, sweep in a south-westerly arc across the horizon. Millions of years ago these hills were truly mountainous with their height, now much eroded by the actions of the Irish weather, once rivalling the European Alps.

Dublin Bay (2003) - Next Page	
Medium:	*Oil on Canvas*
Size:	*1,500mm (Wide) x 1,000mm (High)*
Reference No:	*OL0001*

Standing Stone: *Standing stones were single stone pillars (in Irish known as a Gallán) erected during the Late Neolithic or Early Bronze Age (c.3000BC), usually to mark a burial site, a boundary or an historic event. They were often of immense proportions, perhaps up to 6m high, and would have required both brawn and brains to source, carry to the site and raise to the vertical. Stone pillars were also erected in groups to form a stone alignment or a circle where religious or social ceremonies were carried out. Examples abound in the outer Dublin area, particularly in the hilly regions to the south-west. The example shown here is, however, from Co. Cork, where this artist sketched it when visiting his in-laws.*

Standing Stone (1998)	
Medium:	*Oil on Canvas*
Size:	*600mm (Wide) x 900mm (High)*
Reference No:	*OL0002*

Hiberno Norse Dublin c.1000AD

(Map in full colour on following pages)

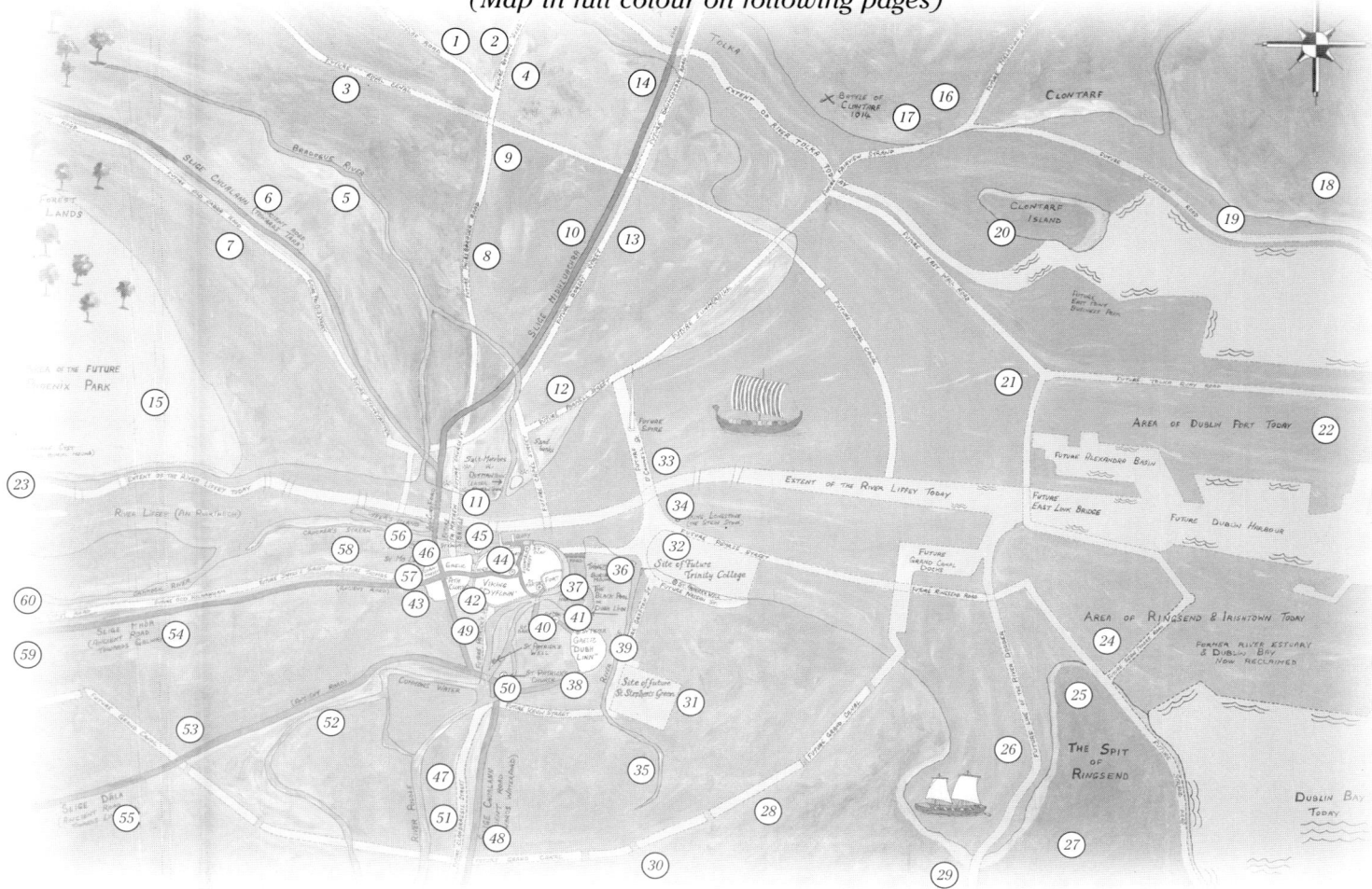

Key to Map (future developments in italics)

1. *Finglas Road*
2. *District of Glasnevin*
3. *Royal Canal*
4. *Botanic Road*
5. Bradogue River
6. Slige Chualann
7. *Old Cabra Road*
8. *Phibsborough Road*
9. *District of Phibsborough*
10. Slige Midhluachra
11. Ostmantown
12. *Parnell Street*
13. *Dorset Street*
14. *District of Drumcondra*
15. *Phoenix Park*
16. *District of Marino*

17. Reputed site of Battle of Clontarf, 1014
18. *District of Clontarf*
19. *Clontarf Road*
20. Clontarf Island
21. *District of East Wall*
22. *Dublin Port Area*
23. *River Liffey*
24. *District of Ringsend*
25. The Spit of Ringsend
26. Ringsend inlet & anchorage
27. *District of Sandymount*
28. *Grand Canal*
29. *District of Ballsbridge*
30. *District of Ranelagh*
31. *St Stephen's Green*

32. *Trinity College (then in the estuary!)*
33. *O'Connell Street*
34. Viking Longstone (Steyne)
35. River Steyne
36. Thingmount
37. Dubh Linn (Black Pool)
38. Monastery & village of Dubh Linn
39. Church of St Peter
40. Church of St Bridget
41. Church of St Mac Táil
42. Viking Dyflinn
43. Village of Ath Cliath
44. Church of St Colm Cille
45. *Fr Mathew Bridge*

46. Hurdle Ford
47. River Poddle
48. Slige Chualann
49. *Patrick Street*
50. St Patrick's Church (later Cathedral)
51. *Clanbrassil Street*
52. Commons Water
53. *District of Dolphin's Barn*
54. Slige Mhór
55. Slige Dála
56. Usher's Island
57. Church of St Mo Lua
58. *Thomas Street*
59. *District of Kilmainham*
60. *District of Islandbridge*

Key to Drawings

1. High Cross of Finglas
2. Knockmaree burial cist, Phoenix Park

3. Bronze Age shield and spears
4. A stone inscribed with ancient Ogham writing

5. Church of St Michael le Pole
6. A Viking Ship
7. Celtic House

8. The Steyne (also Stein or Steine) Stone
9. Excavated Viking artefacts

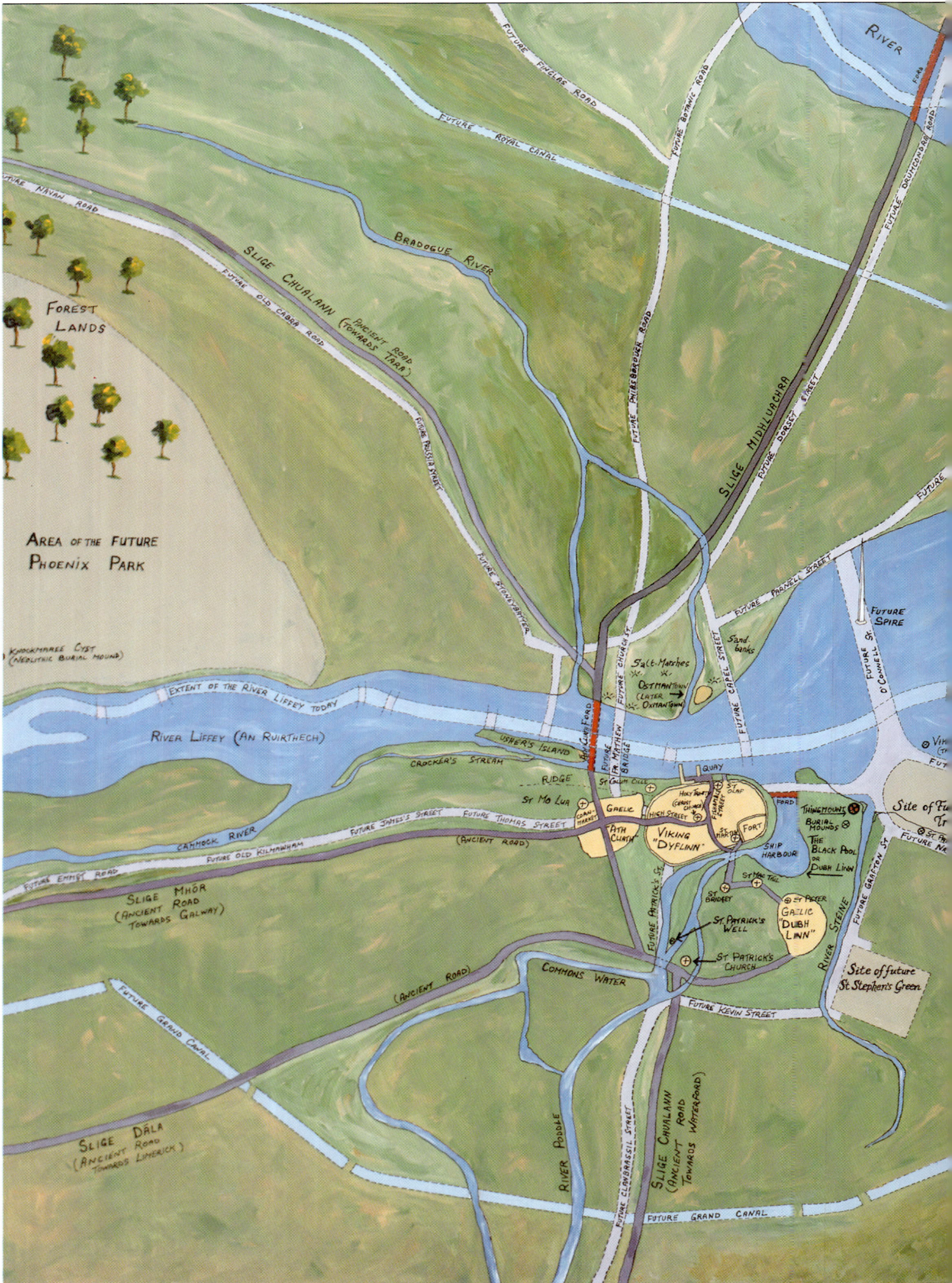

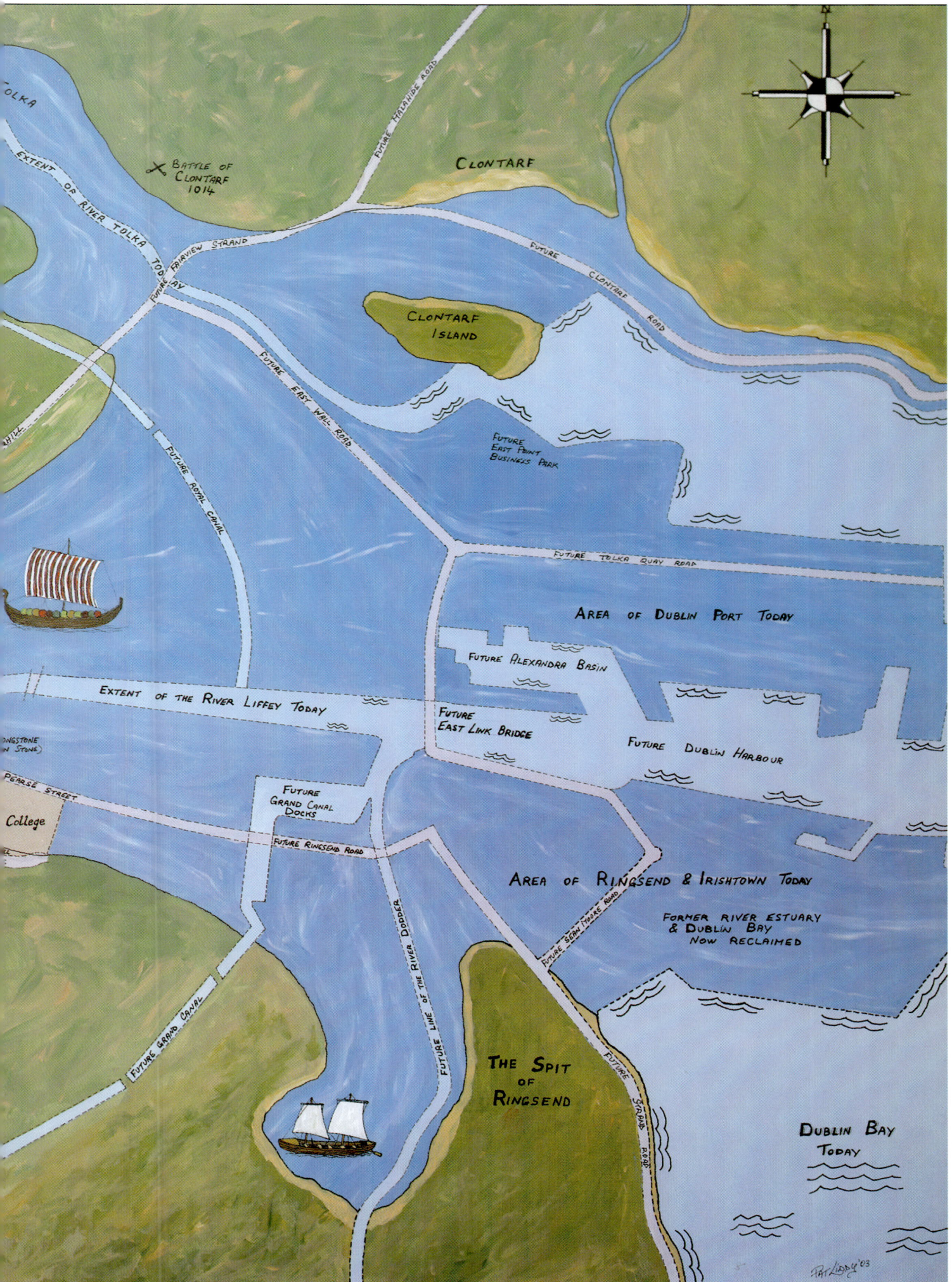

TOLKA

EXTENT OF RIVER TOLKA

FUTURE HOWTH ROAD

BATTLE OF
CLONTARF
1014

CLONTARF

FUTURE FAIRVIEW STRAND

TOLKA BAY

FUTURE EAST WALL ROAD

CLONTARF
ISLAND

FUTURE CLONTARF ROAD

FUTURE ROYAL CANAL

FUTURE
EAST POINT
BUSINESS PARK

FUTURE TOLKA QUAY ROAD

AREA OF DUBLIN PORT TODAY

FUTURE ALEXANDRA BASIN

EXTENT OF THE RIVER LIFFEY TODAY

FUTURE
EAST LINK BRIDGE

FUTURE DUBLIN HARBOUR

LONGSTONE
(N STONE)

PEARSE STREET

College

FUTURE
GRAND CANAL
DOCKS

FUTURE RINGSEND ROAD

AREA OF RINGSEND & IRISHTOWN TODAY

FORMER RIVER ESTUARY
& DUBLIN BAY
NOW RECLAIMED

FUTURE GRAND CANAL

FUTURE LINE OF THE RIVER DODDER

FUTURE SEAN MOORE ROAD

THE SPIT
OF
RINGSEND

FUTURE STRAND ROAD

DUBLIN BAY
TODAY

PatLiddy '03

Hiberno Norse Dublin c.1000AD

(Map in full colour on previous pages)

The intention of this map is to show the layout of the modern city's principal features in relation to the topography of Dublin around 1000AD. Space in this volume unfortunately does not permit a detailed historical treatise on the origins and development of Dublin - for this the reader will have to consult many other fine books written on the subject (some of which are listed in the bibliography section).

Hiberno Norse Dublin c.1000AD (previous pages): The confluence of the River Liffey and the other main rivers formed a wide estuary that began to broaden into the open sea as far west as modern-day Capel Street. The darker blue colour represents the extent of the estuary at high tide in the Viking period and the lighter blue areas delineate the course of today's waterways and coastline after a millennium of land reclamation and development. Some of the modern main roads leading out of the centre of Dublin more or less coincide with the direction, if not the actual line, of the five ancient Celtic national highways (slige) which converged on Dublin. They were originally constructed by the Celts around the second century AD. The Dubh Linn (Black Pool), which provided first the Irish and then the Vikings with a natural safe anchorage, was formed by the River Poddle as it swung northwards to meet the Liffey. It was overlooked by a high ridge which proved ideal as the site for the fortified town established by the Norsemen.

Generally the ground around this ridge was marshy and punctuated by several rivers and streams which further enhanced its defence. These same waterways provided fresh water to the inhabitants and later provided power to many mills. Most of the minor streams, while still existing, have long since been culverted to pour unobserved into the Liffey. Áth Cliath (Hurdle Ford), the ancient ford across the River Liffey, linked the northern slige with their southern counterparts. At this point the hamlet of Áth Cliath (from which the Irish name for Dublin, Baile Átha Cliath, is derived) sprung up. Southeast of Áth Cliath, around the 5th or 6th century, the recently christianised Celts founded the monastery of Dubh Linn which in the normal tradition would have had a village compound built around it. A number of other churches appeared in the surrounding area over the next few centuries. When the Vikings settled in Dublin, despite their ferocious reputation for pillaging monasteries and churches, some modus vivendi appears to have been worked out as the three settlements more or less co-existed with each other. In fact, the

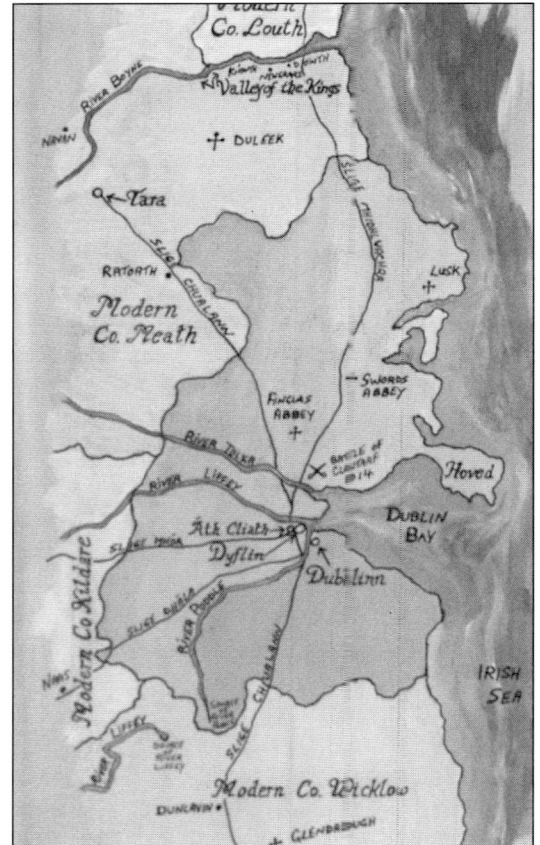

Dublin County c.1000AD: This map of Dublin County and parts of the neighbouring counties shows the location and relative size of Dublin around 1000AD.

Vikings named their town Dyflinn, an obvious adaptation of Dubh Linn. Dyflinn went on to become one of the most important trading seaports in Northern Europe during the 10th and 11th centuries. The always uneasy and sometimes savage relations between the native Celt and the foreign Viking had also a practical side. Celtic produce could now be exported using the established Viking shipping lanes. With notable exceptions (including the Battle of Clontarf in 1014), pragmatism from both sides generally encouraged a working peace between Dyflinn and the hinterland.

Ostmantown, on the northern banks of the Liffey, was a "suburb" of Dyflinn and it was to here that the Viking population moved en masse when they lost their town to the Anglo-Normans in 1170. Ostman translates as the Men from the East (i.e. the Viking). The Thingmount was an artificial hill raised by the Vikings where they held a form of parliament and passed laws. It stood near present-day Suffolk Street.

Hiberno-Norse Map c.1000AD (2003) - Previous Pages	
Medium:	*Acrylic on Wood*
Size:	*1,370mm (Wide) x 1,015mm (High)*
Reference No:	*MP0001*

Steyne Stone: *The Vikings made a significant landfall in Dublin around 841AD and sometime soon after that they stabbed a long stone or Steyne into the mud flats at the outlet of a small tributary of the Liffey. The Steyne (a Norse word) gave its name to the river and to the adjacent area. Placing such a stone was a tradition of the Vikings when they came to settle in a new territory and its purpose was both symbolic (to show that they intended to remain) and practical (as a navigation aid). The River Steyne has since dried up and the ancient stone, which had stood at the same spot somewhere between modern Townsend Street and College Street for hundreds of years, disappeared in the mid-18th century after the district had been reclaimed from the sea. The replacement, which now stands at the junction of Pearse Street with Townsend Street, was erected in 1986. The two head-reliefs represent Ivaar, a Norse king of Dublin at the end of the 9th century, and a nun from the nearby medieval convent of Mary de Hogges. The sculptor was Cliodna Cusson.*

Steyne Stone (2003)	
Medium:	*Pen & Ink on Board*
Size:	*260mm (Wide) x 235mm (High)*
Reference No:	*DR0001*

Viking Dyflinn: When the Vikings set up their first longphort (fortified harbour) around the Dubh Linn (Black Pool - see page 5) and the west end of today's Temple Bar in 841, their encampment was small and disorganised and lacked the more permanent characteristics that would be evident a century later. They parked their boats in the relative shelter of the Dubh Linn and regularly launched aggressive raids on wealthy monasteries in the hinterland which could be reached by river or from the coastline. Gaelic warlords mounted the occasional offensive against them and the Vikings were ousted more than once from their Liffey-side base. In 902 a determined assault expelled the Norse and they remained in exile in Britain for fifteen years. When they returned in strength in 917 they came to stay. Based on the experience they had gained while living in or near Anglo-Saxon villages and towns they proceeded to lay out a more urbanised settlement with agreed boundaries. The houses were in the Gaelic rather than the Anglo-Saxon style which may indicate a co-operative interface with the local communities. To protect their regained properties they erected timber and mud defensive embankments which less than two centuries later would be replaced by stone walls. This reproduction of the early Viking Dyflinn (the name obviously derived from Dubh Linn) was based on the construction of a replica section of the town erected for an exhibition in 1988. The layout of the replica was carefully designed according to findings from extensive archaeological research.

Dyflinn c.1000AD (1992)

Medium:	Pen & Ink on Board
Size:	360mm (Wide) x 217mm (High)
Reference No:	DR0002

Ancient City Walls and St. Audoen's Arch: *St. Audoen's Arch is the last remaining gateway in the city's ancient city walls (see pages 17 - 20). This section of wall was built around 1240 when the River Liffey lapped up against it before reclamation pushed the river further away and required a new defensive line to be built. The wall was thus incorporated into the town centre and houses were eventually built on either side of it. This fact helped to preserve the wall which was subsequently restored and somewhat romantically added to in the 19th century. Further major improvements were carried out in the 1980s. While this section of the medieval city wall along Cook Street is by far the largest intact example there are several other fragmentary parts of the wall standing near to and under Dublin Castle.*

Saint Audeon's Arch (2003)	
Medium:	*Pen & Ink on Board*
Size:	*260mm (Wide) x 235mm (High)*
Reference No:	*DR0003*

Dublin Castle: *Dublin Castle, including the medieval Record Tower, the Chapel Royal and part of the State Apartments, as seen from the south ward, adjacent to the formal gardens.*

Dublin Castle (2003)

Medium:	Pen & Ink on Board
Size:	240mm (Wide) x 290mm (High)
Reference No:	DR0004

Dublin Castle, one of the very oldest institutions in the city, has been altered and reconstructed many times in its history. Following the Anglo-Norman conquest of parts of Ireland in the 1170s the English King John ordered the erection of Dublin Castle in 1204 "…for the safe custody of our treasure, for the administration of justice and for the defence of the city…". By 1230 the construction was completed. It was a medium-sized castle and was integrated into the south-eastern corner of the city walls. The exposed southern and eastern ramparts were protected by a huge moat, 22 metres (72 ft) wide and 12 metres (39 ft) deep. The moat was filled by the River Poddle. Having previously survived a couple of assaults, in 1684 the castle was virtually destroyed by an accidental fire but was largely rebuilt by the early 18th century. The new buildings provided a variety of administration offices, a number of richly decorated rooms for state receptions and residential apartments for the King's deputy in Ireland, the Lord Lieutenant. The latter usually lived in the Vice-Regal Lodge in the Phoenix Park but he did reside in the castle during the so-called Castle Season, a six-week period of entertainment which reached its climax with a Grand Ball on March 17, St Patrick's Day. Young ladies were presented at the levees in the castle in the hope of securing a well-positioned husband. The area enclosed by the Castle was further extended over the years to provide additional facilities. During the Great War of 1914-1918 the apartments (today known as the State Apartments) were pressed into service as a Red Cross Hospital. On 16 January 1922, after the cessation of the War of Independence, the Provisional Government of the Irish Free State received possession of Dublin Castle from the last Lord Lieutenant, Lord FitzAlan. Since then the State Apartments, other ancillary buildings and the Castle's modern Conference Centre are used to host visiting heads of Government, meetings of the European Union, the inauguration of each new President of Ireland, conferences and state tribunals of enquiry. The State Apartments, the Chapel Royal and the Undercroft (the archaeological remains of the old castle) are open to the public.

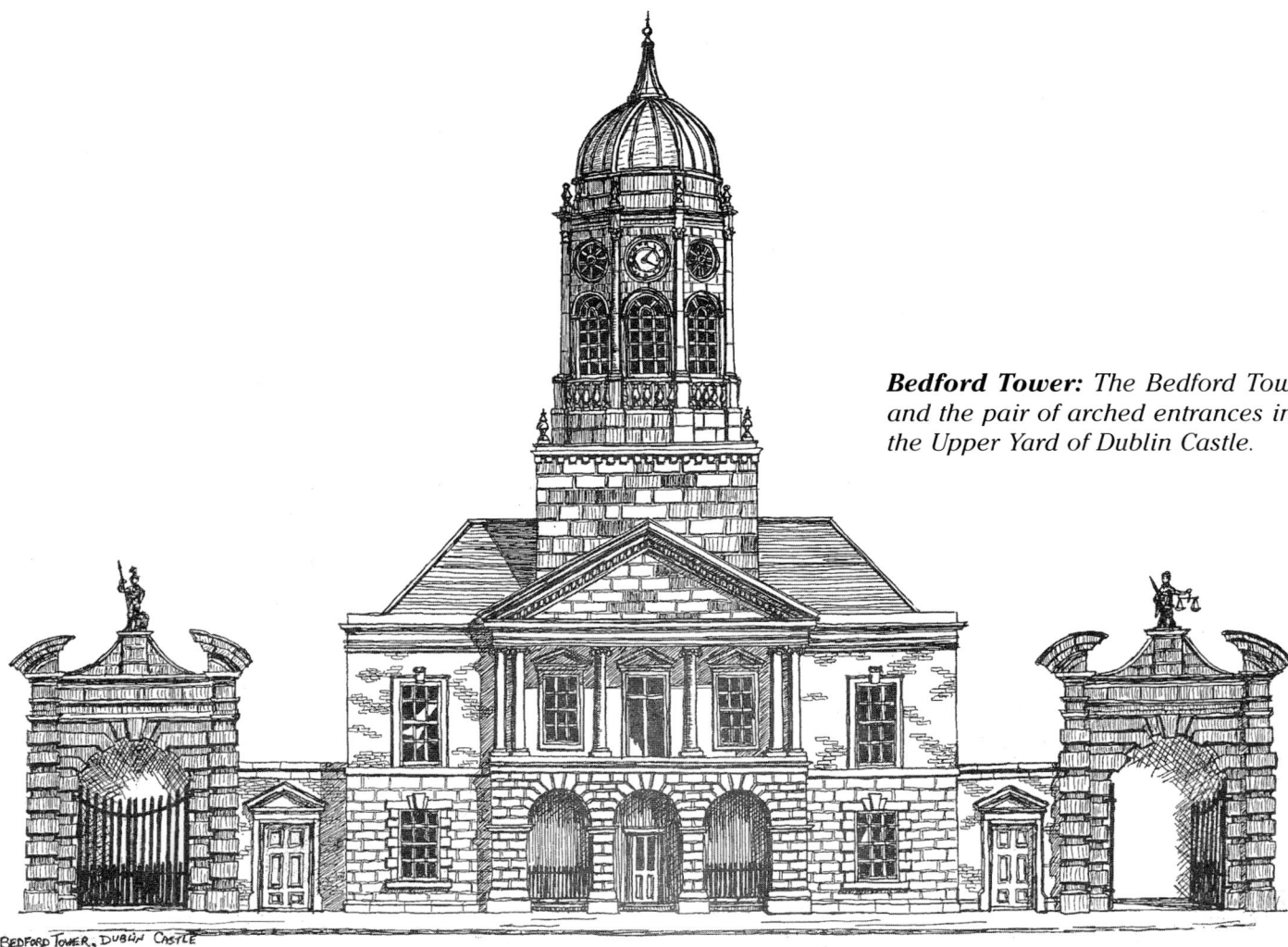

Bedford Tower: *The Bedford Tower and the pair of arched entrances into the Upper Yard of Dublin Castle.*

Bedford Tower *(1998)*	
Medium:	*Pen & Ink on Board*
Size:	*260mm (Wide) x 180mm (High)*
Reference No:	*DR0005*

Lanestown Castle, Newbridge Demesne: *In addition to the large castles that protected the perimeter of Dublin and the surrounding counties, scores of fortified houses were built, particularly during the troubled 14th to the 17th centuries. They usually consisted of a single tower block encircled by a small courtyard and a protective wall. The tower may have had the defensive accoutrements of a large castle such as battlements, machicolations, loopholes and, in rarer cases, a portcullis. The tower houses, commonly but mistakenly called castles, were the homes of Irish chieftains, planters, moderately wealthy landowners, English government officials and such like. Lanestown Castle, which stands on the grounds of Newbridge Demesne, is one such example.*

Lanestown Castle (2001)

Medium:	*Watercolour on Paper*
Size:	*180mm (Wide) x 195mm (High)*
Reference No:	*WC0001*

St. Patrick's Cathedral (2003) - Next Page

Medium:	*Pen & Ink on Board*
Size:	*255mm (Wide) x 235mm (High)*
Reference No:	*DR0006*

Saint Patrick's Cathedral: *The building of St Patrick's Cathedral represented one of the first major high-rise additions to the otherwise low-lying landscape of the fledgling medieval town of Dublin. It was also placed outside of the safety (or suffocating confines, depending on your point of view) of the city walls. The site was once the location of an ancient well where St Patrick is said to have baptised converts in the 5th century. A church was erected here shortly afterwards and was still in use when the Anglo-Normans arrived to Dublin in 1170. Archbishop John Comyn replaced the old Celtic church with a stone one in 1191 and built the nearby palace of St Sepulchre as his new residence. He wished to wean himself away from the influence of the Augustinian Priory attached to Christ Church Cathedral and set up his own independent cathedral. In 1213, his ambition was realised posthumously when St Patrick's was elevated to cathedral status. From 1225 the cathedral was refashioned in the style that we see today. The design of the central part of the church is an almost exact copy of Salisbury Cathedral, which was being built at the same time. Ireland's first university was founded at St. Patrick's in 1320 and intermittently operated for the next 200 years. The cathedral's most famous dean was Jonathan Swift (1667-1745), creator of 'Gulliver's Travels' and indefatigable champion of the many underprivileged who lived in the vicinity of his church. Centuries of financial deprivation and some deliberate abuse (Oliver Cromwell stabled his horses here in 1649) seriously degraded the fabric of the building and it was in danger of imminent collapse until Benjamin Lee Guinness (he of the famous brewery) spent a large fortune on its restoration in the 1860s. The massive west tower, rebuilt by Archbishop Minot in 1370 after a fire, houses the large peal of bells whose ringing tones are so much part of the character of this part of Dublin. One of the city's first clocks was placed on this tower in 1560. The cathedral is open to the public and it would be very worthwhile to attend at one of the daily services when the beautiful singing of the choir can be enjoyed. The Choir School, founded in 1432, is the oldest in the country.*

Christ Church Cathedral: *Hiberno-Norse Dublin received its first major public building when Donat, the first Bishop of Dublin, ordered the construction of his new cathedral church in 1038. Financial support was given by the Norse King of Dublin, Sitric Silkenbeard. In 1163 Archbishop Laurence O'Toole (canonised 1225 and now Patron Saint of the Archdiocese of Dublin) replaced the secular clergy of Christ Church with Augustinian Canons Regular. The ruins of their priory chapter house can still be seen outside the cathedral's south wall. Funded by Strongbow, the Anglo-Norman conqueror of the city, and his companion knights, work commenced in 1172 on replacing the Norse wooden structure with a stone cathedral built in the Norman tradition. Because it took several decades to complete the construction, a variety of architectural styles, from Romanesque to English Gothic, were employed. In 1541 the Augustinian priory was dissolved by Henry VIII and the cathedral became part of the Anglican Community. For exactly 700 years, until the Church of Ireland was disestablished in 1871, Christ Church was the State Church in which senior representatives of the crown swore their oaths of allegiance. Among its great attractions is the Crypt, one of the largest of its kind in these islands, in which are housed many of the treasures of the cathedral. It is an uplifting experience to listen to the choir at Christ Church who perform at most services. Along with that of St Patrick's Cathedral the choir at Christ Church took part in the first ever performance of Handel's 'Messiah' at adjacent Fishamble Street on April 13, 1742.*

Christ Church Cathedral (2003)	
Medium:	Pen & Ink on Board
Size:	355mm (Wide) x 215mm (High)
Reference No:	DR0007

Late Medieval Dublin c.1530

(Map in full colour on following pages)

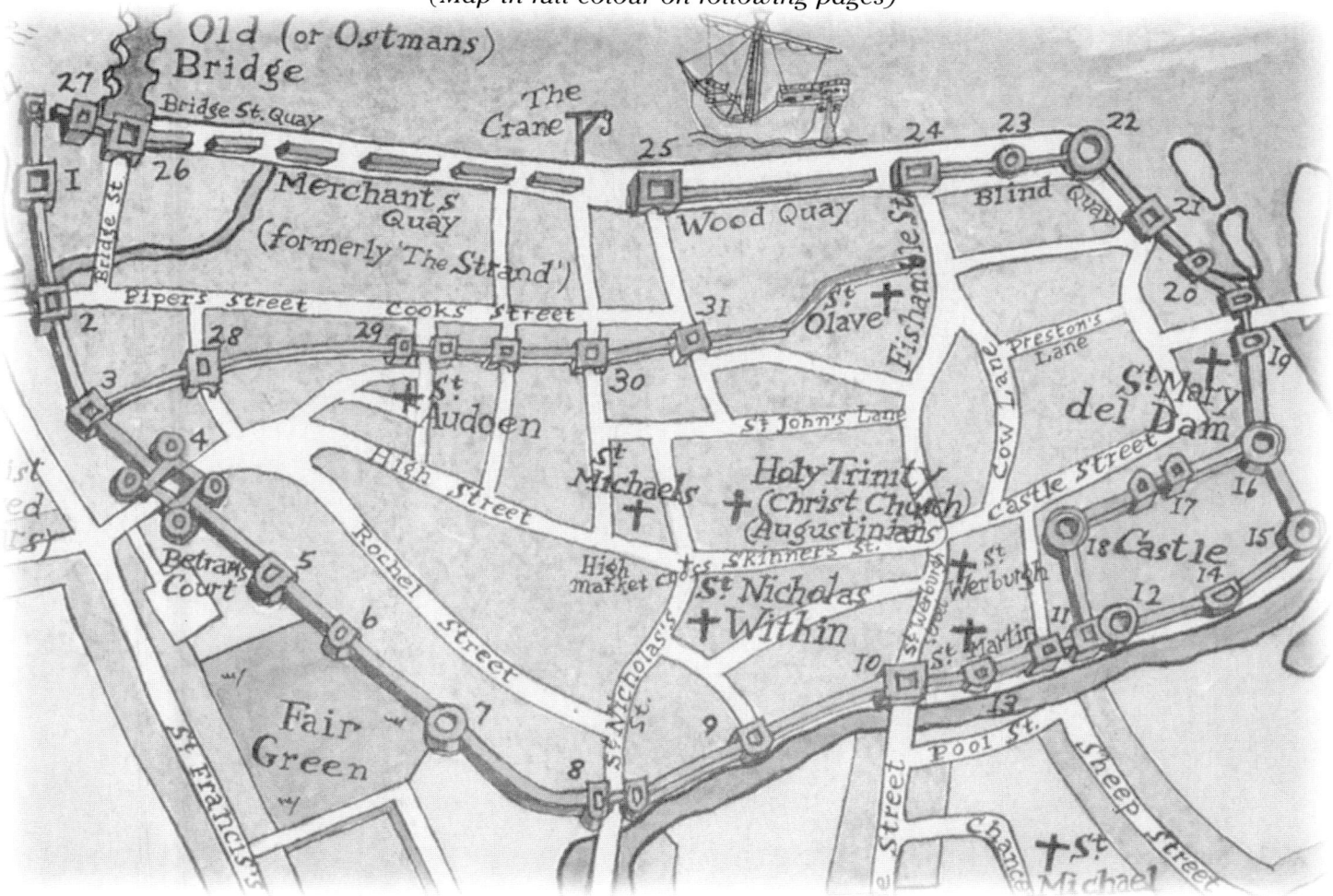

Key to the Gates and Towers along the City Wall

Note: Some of these gates and towers have been named differently over the centuries but the following titles are their most common names.

1. Harbard's Tower	12. Bermingham's Tower	23. Case's Tower
2. Gormand's Gate	13. Stanihusrt's Tower	24. Fyan's Castle
3. The Corner *or* Brown's Tower	14. The Middle Tower	25. Prickett's Tower
4. Newgate	15. Record Tower	26. Bridge or Ostman's gate
5. The Watch Tower	16. Powder Tower	27. Usher's Tower
6. Sedgrave's Tower	17. Castle Gate	28. Fagan's Tower
7. The Round Tower	18. Cork Tower	29. St. Audoen's Gate (still exists)
8. St. Nicholas's Gate	19. Dame's Gate	30. Mac Giollamocholmog's Gate
9. Geneville's Tower	20. Bise's Tower	31. The King's Gate
10. Pole Gate	21. Buttevant's Tower	
11. Austin's Gate	22. Isolde's Tower	

1. Christ Church (before re-building)   2. Saint Patrick's (before re-building)

Oxmantown Green

Oxmantown

Kings Lane

Frapper Lane

Broad St

Smithfield

Lebhome Lane

Comynes Lane

Oxmantown Street

Cow Lane

Colcet Lane

Fisher's Lane

Pill Lane

St Michan's

Haneman Lane

St Saviour's (Dominican's)

River Liffey

Usher's Island

Old (or Ostmans) Bridge

Bridge St. Quay

The Crane

Usher's Pill

27

Bridge St

1   26

Merchants Quay (formerly 'The Strand')

Wood

25

Crockers' Bars (Gate)

Crocker' Street

St John the Baptist (Calced Friars)

Piper's street

2

3

Cooks Street

28   29

31

St Audoen

30

St Michaels

St James's Gate

St Catherine

St Thomas's Street

Katherine St

4

Betraph Court

High Street

High market cross skit

St N W

5

Rochel street

St Nicholas

Cistern

St Thomas (Augustinian Canons)

6

7

9

Fair Green

8

St Francis's Street

St Francis (Franciscan Friars)

St B

City Watercourse

Bon our street

The Coombe

St Francis's Gate

St Patrick's Gate

St Patrick's Street

New Street

Commons Water

River Poddle

New Street Gate

River Bradogue

N

Subject to flooding

Future Spire

Line of High Tide

St Mary's
(Cistercians)
St Mary's Abbey

Longstone   St James

Holly Trinity

Steine
& Mill

Recently reclaimed
from the sea
Subject to flooding

24 23 22

Blind Gate   21

All
Saints
(Augustinian
Canons)

Fishamble St
20
19   St Andrew

Cow Lane
Prestons
Lane
St Mary
del Dam

Thingmount

high
this   18 17 16
St
Werburgh   St Castle 15
14

Castle Street

St Paul

St
Martin   12

13   St George

St Mary de
Hogges
(Arroasia'n Nuns)

15

Pool St
Sheep Street
Fool St

St Georges Lane

Crosse Lane

Chancellors Lane

St
Michael
le Pole

St Stephen's Street

St Peter
Whitefriars'
Gate

St Stephen's
(Leper Hospital)

St Mary
(Carmelite)
Friars

St Stephen's Green

hbishop's
lace of
Sepulchre

River Steine

St Kevin's
Gate

St
Kevin

Drawn by Pat Liddy © 2003 and largely based on
the research of Dr. Howard Clarke & Prof. Anngret Simms
and John Speed's map of 1610 and many other sources

Late Medieval Dublin c.1530

(Map in full colour on previous pages)

Late Medieval Dublin c.1530 (previous pages): *In the 360 years since the Anglo-Norman conquest of Dublin the town had developed and grown somewhat but not as much as might have been expected given the organisational abilities of its conquerors and the importance attached to Dublin by the English crown. Many events, however, conspired against any substantial growth including a series of devastating plagues which hit Dublin during the 14th and 15th centuries. English investment in, and trade with, Dublin, upon which the town largely depended, was severely curtailed due to Anglo-Scottish and Anglo-French wars and power struggles in England itself. The constant threat of war as well as actual raids and sieges made citizens apprehensive to develop suburbs too far from the safety of the walls. The same walls were expanded towards the new waterfront when the Liffey's width was once more shortened to create anchorage for deeper-draft vessels. The length of wall left behind, clearly outlined on the map, survived when the rest of the ramparts were later demolished. A large section of that inner wall is still visible along Cook Street.*

Most of the built-up areas around the outskirts of the enclosed town were in fact those associated with the religious orders. But even these settlements received a severe blow when in the late 1530s all the monasteries, abbeys and convents were closed on the orders of Henry Vlll. Not that initially the population were sorry to see them shut down as many people had grown envious of the supposed temporal wealth of these institutions but with their closure went the city's only hospitals and social services, a deficit that would not be made up for a couple of centuries.

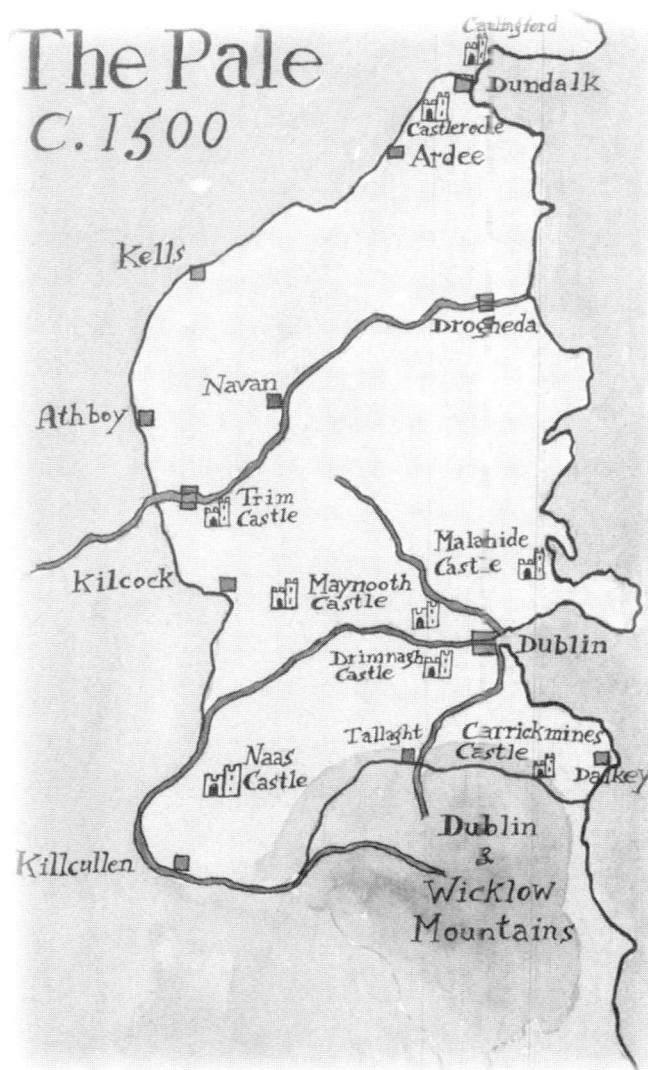

The Pale: *The Pale was the name given to the region around Dublin which remained more or less under the control of the English. Its extent during the periods leading up to the time of Elizabeth l shrank or expanded in accord with the political and military situations of the day.*

Late Medieval Dublin c.1530 *(2003)* - Previous Pages	
Medium:	*Line & Watercolour*
Size:	*680mm (Wide) x 495mm (High)*
Reference No:	*WC0101*

Dublin 1610 by John Speed

(Map in full colour on following pages)

Dublin 1610 by John Speed (following pages): *The Ireland of the late 16th and early 17th century was a very troubled land beset as it was by religious and colonial wars. Dublin's crumbling old city walls, towers and gateways were restored and strengthened but the life in the town more or less stagnated. In about 1605 a surveyor visited Dublin to prepare John Speed's famous, and now Dublin's earliest surviving, map. 'Dubline', dated 1610 and published a year later as an insert on the Leinster folio page of 'Theatre of the Empire of Great Britaine', certainly gives us an insight into early Jacobean Dublin. There are some inaccuracies as regards exaggerated street widths, standardised house and church types and too many open spaces but the general extent shown of the town, its defensive walls and towers and the growing suburbs is reliable. Except in the case of some names (e.g. St Thomas Court and St Mary's Abbey) and the remains of boundary walls, all traces of the suppressed abbeys and convents have disappeared. The great Priory of All Hallows has been replaced by Trinity College. This institution received its first students in 1594 and had as its expressed policy a mission to convert the Irish from Popery (see page 34). It must be remembered that the size of the original map was tiny, being only 15cm x 17cm, so there is an excuse for the paucity of topographical detail.*

DUBLINE
1610

St Mi cham
Church
St Marys Lane
St Marys Abbey
The Bridge Street
Pill Lane
The Inn
The Bridge Gate
Fians Castle
Newmans st
Wood Key
Merchant's Key
Rame Lane
Bridge Street
Cooke Street
Merchant Street
Ormonde Gate
School House
St Michaels Lane
St Winifred
Fish Shambles st
Dames Gate
The Mills
New Rowe
Johns House
Newgate
Kayes Merchant Street
St Owens ch
St Mich
St Iohns ch
Christ Church
Castle street
St Werbo Church
High Street Thatholeth
Skinners
The Castle
St Thomas Street
Back Lane
St Nicholas Church
St Catherins Ch
St Francis Street
St Nicholas Street
St Nicholas G
Brides Church
Brides Street
Sheepe Street
St Michal le Pole
St Iames's Street
St Thom Court
Crosse Lane
St Patricks Street
New River
St Patricks ch
St Sepulchers
The Come
Church on Paul
St Kevan St

50   100   150   200
A Scale of Paces

St Augustines

The Hospital

ames Street

Bridewell

The Colledge

Georges Lane

St Stevens
gh

St Stevens Street

St Peters
Church

St Stevens
Church

te Friers

Ancient Seal of Dublin, 1459.

Speed Map 1610: *Original map of John Speed, published in 1610 and redrawn and hand-coloured by Pat Liddy 2003.*

Speed Map 1610 (2003)

Medium:	Line & Watercolour
Size:	479mm (Wide) x 396mm (High)
Reference No:	WC010

'Dutch Billies', Dublin

Pat Liddy Sep'00

Dutch Billies: *In the evolving history of Dublin the most characteristic streetscape throughout the 17th and much of the 18th century, especially along thoroughfares not re-developed in the Georgian idiom, was that formed by the so-called 'Dutch Billy' front-gabled building. This style was introduced into Ireland in the 1600s by Flemish and Dutch immigrant craftsmen. The nickname is derived from King William of Orange, the Dutch-born royal who secured his claim to the English throne by defeating James ll at the battles of the Boyne (1690) and Aughrim (1691). From an original stock of thousands only a handful of genuine 'Dutch Billies' remain in the city today although several new apartment complexes echo the style in their gable finishes. The survivors featured here are situated on (from the left); Kevin Street, Molesworth Street, Duke Street and Leeson Street.*

Dutch Billies (2000)	
Medium:	*Line & Watercolour*
Size:	*256mm (Wide) x 140mm (High)*
Reference No:	*WC011*

Malahide Castle: *As a reward for loyalty and to help secure Ireland for the English crown, Henry II granted the lands of Malahide to Sir Richard Talbot. In 1185 Talbot moved into his new castle which was to remain in the family's hands until the death of Milo Talbot in 1973 when the property had to be sold to defray taxes. Fortunately the castle was purchased by the then Dublin County Council and both it and the surrounding lands are now open to the public. Today's castle bears little resemblance to the original 12th century fortress as the structure was adapted and enlarged several times over the centuries. One of the towers, however, is believed to date from the 13th century. The surrounding curtain walls also disappeared over time.*

Malahide Castle *(1988)*	
Medium:	*Watercolour on Paper*
Size:	*445mm (Wide) x 345mm (High)*
Reference No:	*WC0104*

Dunsoghly Castle

Bradoge River

Oxmantown River

Ashtown Castle

Phoenix Park

Bowling Green

Royal Hospital Kilmainham

River Liffey

Sir William Usher's Island

Camac River

Lazy Hill

Trinity College

Damas Street

Castle

St. Michans

City Walls

St Andrews

1534

The Coombe

Ne Row

New Street

St Stephen's Green

Kilmainham Village

Drimnagh Castle

Dolphins Barn Village

River Poddle

Harolds Cross Village

Rathfarnham Castle

Battle Rathmine

Tolka River

Clondra Castle

Artaine Castle

Malahide Castle

Clontarf Castle

N

Howth Castle

Clontarf Island

High-Tide Coastline

Rings End

Design for Citadel

Ringsend Village

Baggotrath Castle

Simonscourt Castle

Donnybrook Village

649

Pat Liddy 2003

27

Restoration Dublin c.1680

(Map in full colour on previous pages)

Restoration Dublin c.1680 (previous pages): *Having gathered some momentum in the early 17th century the development of Dublin received a serious setback with the insurrection of 1641 in which Irish Catholics, both 'Old English' and native, revolted against English Protestant authority. The commencement of the Civil War in England brought further confusion, with the Catholics warring first against the Royalists and then against the Parliamentarians. The Catholics never managed to capture Dublin but the occupying Royalists lost the city to Oliver Cromwell's forces in 1647. Two years later the former Viceroy, the Duke of Ormond, failed in his attempt to recapture Dublin at the Battle of Rathmines. A short while later Cromwell himself landed at Ringsend in the company of 12,000 Roundhead troops and proceeded to occupy the city causing a great deal of wanton destruction.*

Cromwell's downfall and the restoration of Charles ll brought relief to the fortunes of Dublin. The Duke of Ormonde (he now added the 'e' to the end of his title) was, on his return from Paris, again appointed the King's Viceroy and he immediately set about improving and expanding the city. He enabled a new breed of speculative developers to commence operations and under his personal direction new quays (Ormond Quay, Arran Quay etc) were laid down as well as new streets leading off from them. He ordered that the buildings along the quays should be set back the distance of a street and face the river which was contrary to the normal but foul practice of building the rear of houses right up to the riverfront so that domestic refuse and sewage could be conveniently cast into the waters. He also laid out the new Phoenix Park as a royal hunting ground and established the Royal Hospital as a home for retired and sick soldiers.

Several of the city's rivers, which were later culverted, still flowed above ground. They included the Oxmantown, Bradoge (Bradogue) and Poddle. The Liffey's estuary was still very broad just beyond Trinity College but reclamation reclaimed much of it over the next 50 or 60 years. Suburban villages began to develop with the security of peace now assured in the outlying regions. In this drawing there is included a plan for an impressive star-shaped citadel which was to have been built in the area of Ringsend. This design appears on several maps of the period as there was an official desire to build such a redoubt but the scheme never got off the ground.

Restoration Dublin c.1680 *(2003)* - Previous Pages	
Medium:	Line & Watercolour
Size:	680mm (Wide) x 495mm (High)
Reference No:	WC0102

Dublin 1728

(Map in full colour on following pages)

Dublin 1728 (following pages): *The map, based on that drawn by Charles Brooking, grandly entitled "A Map of the City and Suburbs of Dublin and also the Archbishop and Earl of Meath's Liberties with the bounds of each Parish", was originally published in London by John Bowles in 1728. It included a panorama of Dublin, on the same scale as the map itself, entitled "A Prospect of the City of Dublin from the North". In this and in the directional presentation of the main plan it is unusual, if not confusing, as most other maps of Dublin are positioned with north placed on the top i.e. with the Liffey flowing towards the right-hand side. This was the first map of the city to be produced on its own without being part of a larger map. Illustration of several of Dublin's more notable buildings and statues were bordered around the map but these are not shown here. The Liffey has been further restrained by extensive land reclamations almost as far as Ringsend with consequent deeper shipping channels. This new land was still subject to flooding especially during high tide.*

Apart from the obvious decorative merits of the map it is also highly detailed and informative. The expansion and embellishment of the city, commenced in the 1660s, continued apace and now entered into its Georgian era with the continuing move eastwards onto reclaimed land. Propertied and titled classes began to occupy these new developments leaving their former residences in the old city to be turned into tenements. Although several street names have been changed in modern times many are still recognisable today even if the spellings are in an antiquated form.

The skyline of the compressed panorama is punctuated by the towers and steeples of buildings which, in the main, survive today. The northside of the city is relatively rural while the Dublin Mountains form the backdrop in the distance. At one time there were several windmills in Dublin and three examples are shown towards the left of the picture. Several current streets and roads in Dublin bear testimony to the presence of windmills including Windmill Lane off City Quay. There is yet one surviving windmill in Dublin. Although shorn of its sails it remains the largest one ever built in these islands. Capped by an onion-shaped dome and a wind vane in the image of St Patrick, it stands just off Thomas Street in the area designated for the new Digital Hub complex.

Dublin 1728 *(2003)* - Following Pages		
Medium:	*Line & Watercolour*	
Size:	*1,020mm (Wide) x 640mm (High)*	
Reference No:	*WC0103*	

A MAP of the CITY and Suburbs of DUBLIN And also t

To his Excellency
JOHN Lord CARTERET
Baron of HAWNES one of the Lords
of His MAJESTIES Most Honourable
PRIVY COUNCIL & Lord LIEUTENANT
GENERAL and GENERAL GOVERNOUR
of His MAJESTIES Kingdom of
IRELAND
This Map is Humbly Dedicated
by Charles Brooking
1728.

Brook River

P

The River Liffe

Part is Walled in but as yet

over flow'd by y.e Tide

St John Rogersons Key

Hanover Street

Lime Street

St

St Georges K

Mole Street

La

ze

P

A

M

St

1 Rings End
2 The new Library
3 The College
4 The Round Church
5 The Castle
6 The Tholsel
7 St Patricks Ch.
8 St Warburghs
9 Christ Church
10 St John's
11 St Michael's
12 St Luke's
13 St John's in Thomas St
14 St Catherine's
15 St James's
16 The Poor House
17 The Royal Hospital

THE STRAND

Abbot Street

M

A

hand-coloured & additional
named - Pat Liddy-2003

ARCH BISHOP and EARL of MEATHS Liberties with the bound

PART OF THE BISHOPS LI

St Kevans Church

St Stevens Green

Cuffe Street

St Kevans

Great Butter Lane

ARCH

Susky Street

Stable Lane

York Street

St Peters Street

Wood Street

St Patricks Church

Patricks Alley

Padd

New

St

ST ANNS

PARISH

Molesworth Street

Kildare Street

Mercers House

St Anns Church

Dawson Street

St Patricks Well Lane

ARCH PARISH

William Street

Kildare Street

Anger Street

Chequer Lane

St BRIDGETS PARISH

Great Ship Street

Chancery Lane

St NICH

Trinity

Colledge

Colledge Green

St ANDREWS PARISH

Dame Street

CASTLE

NICHOLAS WITHIN PARISH

Skinners Row

WITH

Francis Street

St Nich

College Street

Dame Street

Georges Street

Cork Hill

Warburgs

Castle Street

High Street

ST MICHAEL PARISH

St Audons Church

Hawkins Street

Fleet Street

Temple Bar

WARBURGHS PARISH

JOHNS

Wine Tavern Street

High Street

STAU DO

Hill

Altons Key

Custom House Key

Essex Street

Wood Key

Merchants Key

Essex Bridge

Ormond Bridge

Old Bridge

Batchelours Walke

Ormond Key

The Inns

Strand Street

Swifts Row

Abby Street

St Marys Abby

ST MICANS PARISH

St Micans Church

New Church

Henry Street

St Marys Street

St Maggs Church

MARYS PARISH

Great Marlborough Street

Bolton Street

Linnen Hall

King Street

Chan el Row

Smith Field

Church

31

...ns of each PARISH. Drawn from an Actual SURVEY Made by Charles B

A Scale of 80 Perch

7 Yards to a Perch

EXPLANATION,
The CITY Liberty
The ARCH BISHOP and
EARL of MEATHS Liberties
are parted by a Water Course
from the Black Pitts to the
Pottle
The Bounds of y Parishes.
A The Four Courts. B. St Nicholas Church
C. St Michaels Church. D. The Playhouse

LIBERTY

St LUKE'S PARISH

THERINES PARISH

PARISH

Coopers Rest

New Row

St Lukes Church

New Market

Mill Street

Chamber St

Cloach Worke

Ormond St

Square

Cork Street

Mutton L

Crooked Staff

Coomb

NHOLAS

St

CATHERINES

Garden Land

Swift Alley

Meath Street

Coles Ally

Thomas

Court

Elbow Lane

Thomas

Barr Street

PARISH

City Bason

Dolphins Barn

The Corn Market House

St Johns Castle

New Row

St Thomas's Street

Hanover Street

St James's Gate

ST

ES'S

Poor House

Royal Hospi

OUT

ONS PARISH

Arran Bridge

Key

Bloody Bridge

Barrack

Street

St PAULS

Oxman Town Green

Bar racks

Church

St JAM

St James's Street

St James's Church

Dr Steevens Hospital

Infirmary

Montpelier Hill

Park Gate

Ha

PARISH

The Way to Island Bridge

Royal Hospital, Kilmainham: *This view through one of the archways of the courtyard of the former Royal Hospital, now the Irish Museum of Modern Art (IMMA), echoes the form of a medieval monastic cloister. In fact the arcaded walkways had a similar purpose to their religious counterparts in that they provided shelter to the residents while taking their exercise. These erstwhile residents were the retired soldiers of the English army for whom the building was opened in 1684. James Butler, Duke of Ormonde and Viceroy to Charles ll, had seen Les Invalides in Paris and decided to set up a similar institution in Dublin. Thus the Royal Hospital became the world's second oldest military retirement home. The last old soldier left in 1928 and the building then fell into disrepair. Between 1980 and 1984 it was completely restored by the government and given over as an art exhibition centre for permanent and visiting exhibitions. Concerts are regularly held in the sumptuous Chapel or in the Great Hall. The building of the Royal Hospital was important as it was Ireland's first major classical public building which began the renaissance of Dublin's architectural landscape under the inspired direction of the Duke of Ormonde.*

Royal Hospital, Kilmainham (2003)

Medium:	*Pen & Ink on Board*
Size:	*260mm (Wide) x 238mm (High)*
Reference No:	*DR010*

Trinity College: *Apart from abbeys, monasteries, a number of parish churches and a scattering of houses, Trinity College was one of the first bold moves by a major institution to locate outside the security of the ancient city walls. Founded in 1592 on the confiscated lands of an Augustinian monastery suppressed in the 1530s by King Henry VIII, the college, and the buildings which arose around it, formed the most easterly expansion of the city to date. Unfortunately nothing of the fabric survives from the 16th century. The Long Room in the Old Library is a direct descendant of Trinity's first library. The building was designed by Thomas Burgh and was formally opened in 1732. The Long Room contains over 200,000 volumes dating from the 16th century as well as ancient Greek and Latin manuscripts, Egyptian papyrus and even a first folio of Shakespeare. It also displays the elaborately crafted Irish Harp which was presented to the College in the 18th century. Although legend ascribes it to the High King, Brian Boruma, who was slain at the Battle of Clontarf in 1014, it is generally believed to be between 500 and 600 years old. The official emblem of Ireland (which, for instance, appears on the country's coinage) was copied from this harp. The library's greatest treasure is its collection of early Irish medieval manuscripts. The single greatest jewel in the possession of Trinity College must be the incomparable Book of Kells. Considered to be the most beautiful illustrated manuscript in the world, its 680 pages of vellum contain the Latin texts of the Four Gospels. It was written c.800AD in a monastery, most likely on the island of Iona, close to the Scottish mainland. It eventually ended up in Kells (Co. Meath) and from there it was deposited for safe keeping in Trinity around 1653.*

Trinity College (2003)	
Medium:	*Pen & Ink on Board*
Size:	*358mm (Wide) x 216mm (High)*
Reference No:	*DR011*

Trinity College West Front: *Another view of the façade of the college, the West Front, was constructed in the 1750s to the designs of an amateur architect, Theodore Jacobsen, who had also designed the London Foundling Hospital. Visitors may freely wander throughout the extensive and evocative grounds of the college.*

Trinity College *(2003)*

Medium:	*Line & Watercolour on Paper*
Size:	*500mm (Wide) x 370mm (High)*
Reference No:	*PR010*

Custom House: *Over the centuries there have been several successive Custom Houses serving the harbour of Dublin (the latest one was opened in 2003 in the Dublin Port complex). The most famous Custom House, and arguably the most impressive of the classical Georgian buildings in the city, is James Gandon's masterpiece on Custom House Quay. Due to space restrictions on docking facilities further upriver, John Beresford, the then Revenue Commissioner, determined in the 1780s to build a new Custom House nearer to the mouth of the River Liffey. He persuaded one of England's most promising architects to pass over an invitation to build in Russia and come to Dublin instead. James Gandon has left Dublin a number of important architectural legacies, not the least of which is his Custom House which was completed by 1792 at a staggering cost then of nearly a quarter of a million pounds. Innovative for its day, its foundations were laid on a bed of wool and wickerwork to counteract the marshy ground of the reclaimed sloblands. In 1921, during the War of Independence, the Custom House was attacked by the IRA and fell prey to a disastrous fire. The conflagration was so intense that the stone rubble was still cooling weeks later. Reconstruction appeared hopeless and the building that had inspired Lutyen's Viceroy's Palace in New Delhi seemed doomed. However, the basic walls were still standing so it was decided to proceed with the restoration. The dome and drum had to be totally rebuilt. Ireland's best known architectural glory was saved but in the late 1970s and 80s it became apparent that there was serious deterioration to the outer stone fabric caused by problems relating to the earlier fire. Major repair, replacement and conservation works were undertaken from 1984 to 1991 at a cost of around £6 million (€7.6 million). The work was awarded the Europa Nostra Diploma of Merit in 1989. The Visitor Centre has marvellous displays on the history of the building, its function as a custom house and its role as the main centre for administering relief during the tragic famines of the 1840s.*

Custom House (2003)	
Medium:	*Pen & Ink on Board*
Size:	*258mm (Wide) x 216mm (High)*
Reference No:	*DR012*

Custom House, Dublin

Pat Liddy '87

Royal Arms of Ireland: *The Royal Arms of Ireland above the parapet of the Custom House. This and the other carvings around the building were executed by Ireland's greatest 18th century sculptor, Edward Smyth.*

Royal Arms of Ireland *(1987)*	
Medium:	*Pen & Ink on Board*
Size:	*228mm (Wide) x 178mm (High)*
Reference No:	*DR013*

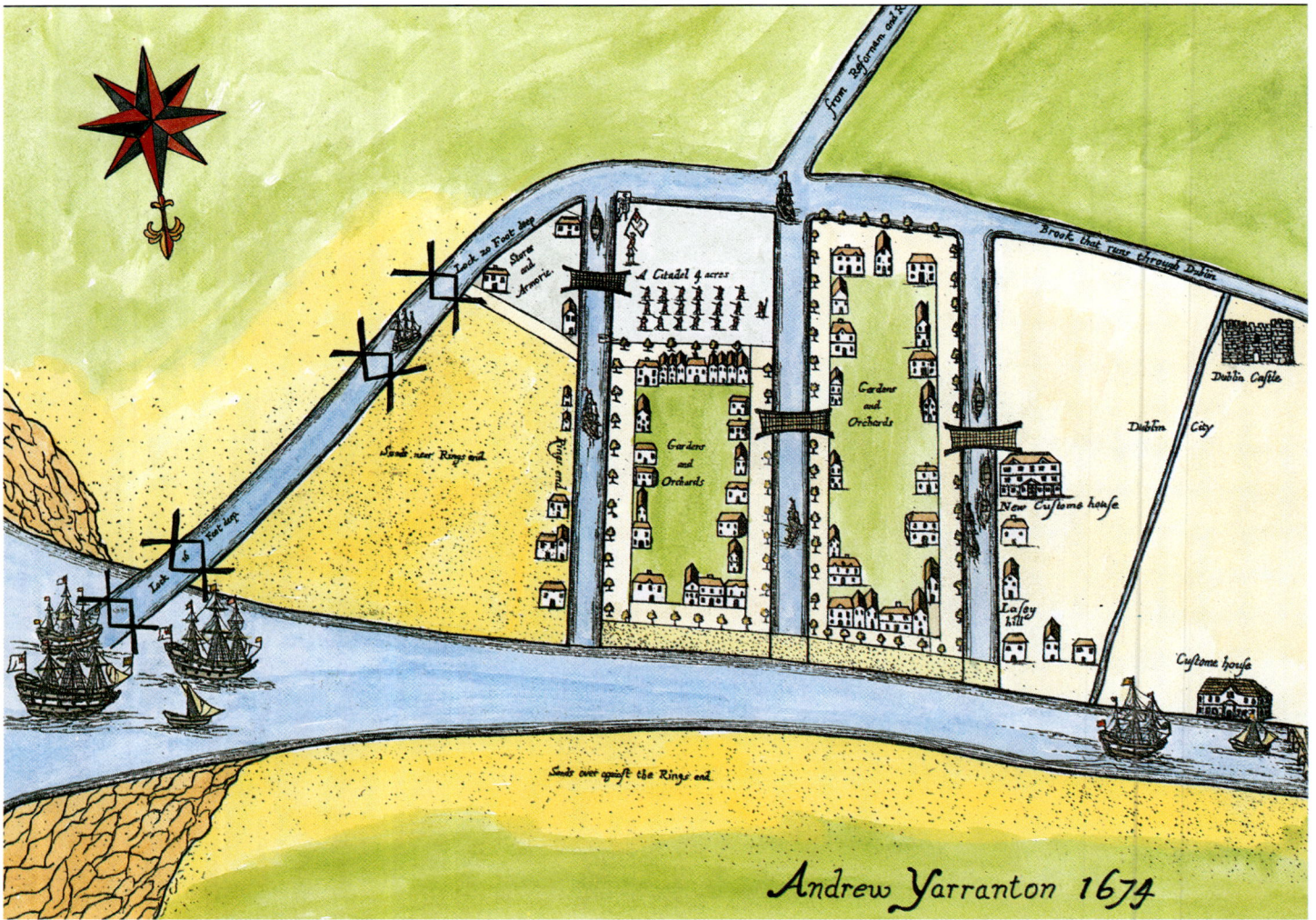

Andrew Yarranton 1674

1674 Map of Dublin by Andrew Yarranton: *This curious little map was originally drawn by Andrew Yarranton, an English businessman, when he visited Dublin in 1674. A terrible storm occurred during his stay and many ships were lost and damaged in the bay and in the then inadequate harbour. The Lord Mayor asked him to draw up a design for a new and safer harbour and this Yarranton did with some imagination. Like many plans for the city in the past and, no doubt, will happen in the future, his proposed scheme came to nought. His ideas were quite visionary in a way as he anticipated a canal system in much the same area where, a hundred years later, the Grand Canal Docks system was developed. Yarranton included a proposed military citadel in the Ringsend district, a feature several more map-makers over the next fifty years were also encouraged to insert by the authorities of the day (also see pages 26/27). This version of the map was redrawn and hand-coloured by the author.*

1674 Map (2003)

Medium:	Line & Watercolour on Paper
Size:	375mm (Wide) x 252mm (High)
Reference No:	WC026

Jewish Cemetery, Fairview

Pat Liddy Sep'00

The Jewish Cemetery, Ballybough: *The arrival of foreign migrants into Dublin is not a new phenomenon as the following piece will show. The plaque over the doorway of a house on Fairview Strand, Ballybough, on Dublin's northside curiously states 'Built in the year 5618'. Rather than presenting some fantastic leap into the future the date actually refers to the Jewish calendar and is equivalent to the year 1857 in the Christian dating system. The cemetery behind the house was established in 1718 to service the 2,000 or so Jews who had migrated from Spain and Portugal to escape religious persecution around 1660. First settling in Crane Lane part of the community later moved to Annadale, a neighbourhood adjacent to the present cemetery. This general area, then closer to the sea than today, also attracted other religious groups who experienced oppression in their homelands including Huguenots and Quakers. The last interment in Ballybough took place in 1908. In the 19th century there was a further wave of Jewish immigration, this time to escape from Russia. This later influx mostly settled on the south side of the city.*

Jewish Cemetery (2000)	
Medium:	*Watercolour on Paper*
Size:	*156mm (Wide) x 126mm (High)*
Reference No:	*WC012*

Guinness Brewery (2003) - Next Page	
Medium:	*Pen & Ink on Board*
Size:	*250mm (Wide) x 285mm (High)*
Reference No:	*DR101*

The Guinness Brewery: *Guinness is the sole remaining large-scale brewing firm in a city that once was home to scores of breweries and distilleries which in the 18th and 19th centuries employed thousands of people. Some of the buildings, including large stone warehouses, that formerly housed these enterprises, still exist and have been converted into new uses including apartments. The world-famous Guinness beverage was first produced in Dublin in 1759 by Arthur Guinness at St James's Gate Brewery later to become the largest brewery in the world. It is no longer that as the Guinness brands are now brewed in many locations around the world and mechanisation has reduced the early 20th century workforce of over 5,000 to less than 800 today. The Guinness family, so long associated with the firm, is no longer involved with the company which is now owned by Diageo. A visit to St James's Gate is still a marvellous experience where modern facilities are surrounded by the impressive and ornate architecture of the Victorian period. One such building is the old Storehouse which now contains the Guinness Visitor Centre where the history and the story of the manufacture of Guinness is told. On the top floor of the Storehouse is the glazed and circular Gravity Bar where visitors may imbibe their complimentary Guinness while gazing down on the city from the one of the best vantage points in town. The Guinness Storehouse, completed in 1904 to house the fermentation process, is one of Dublin's most remarkable industrial buildings reminiscent of the late 19th century buildings of the Chicago School. It is a massive structure rising to an equivalent height of nine storeys. Although the outer walls are of brick the structural framing is of steel. The designer was A.H. Hignett, an engineer employed by Guinness. As well as containing the Visitor Centre, the Guinness Storehouse provides state-of-the-art training facilities, a company archive, a hospitality suite and an exhibition gallery.*

The Halfpenny Bridge: Up to 1816, the year the Halfpenny Bridge was erected, no other bridge existed between Essex (formerly Grattan, also known as Capel Street) Bridge and Carlisle (O'Connell) Bridge. There was a ferry from the Bagnio Slip (at the bottom of Fownes Street) operated by William Walsh. He owned seven leaky ferries and was under pressure from Dublin Corporation to repair them or replace them. He balked at that idea, preferring instead to build a bridge. His proposal to Dublin Corporation was adopted and he was allowed a hundred-year lease during which he could charge a halfpenny toll. Until recently the toll platforms stood at either end of the bridge. Designed by John Windsor and costing £3,894.7s.11d., (in 'old money', i.e. sterling, this means, for those too young to remember pre-decimal coinage, 3,894 pounds, 7 shillings and 11 pence), the bridge was manufactured in Coalbrookdale in Shropshire, the first centre of iron casting in Britain. Now one of the oldest cast-iron bridges in the world it was originally named Wellington Bridge, after the Dublin born duke who had trounced Napoleon at Waterloo. Now called Liffey Bridge, it is more commonly known as the Halfpenny or Ha'penny Bridge. It was reopened in 2002 after undergoing a massive refurbishment in which many rusted or worn sections were faithfully replaced. The bridge was then repainted in an off-white colour to match its original decor. A century ago the city authorities mooted a proposal to remove the bridge as it was thought to be hideous structure. Better councils prevailed and it has since taken on the mantle of being a city symbol.

Halfpenny Bridge (2003)	
Medium:	Pen & Ink on Board
Size:	358mm (Wide) x 216mm (High)
Reference No:	DR015

The Halfpenny Bridge: *The Ha'penny Bridge, viewed from Bachelors' Walk (see also page 41).*

Halfpenny Bridge (2003)

Medium:	*Line & Watercolour*
Size:	*383mm (Wide) x 286mm (High)*
Reference No:	*WC013*

Railway Bridge, Malahide *(2000)*

Medium:	*Line & Watercolour*
Size:	*192mm (Wide) x 183mm (High)*
Reference No:	*WC014*

Railway Bridge, Malahide: The arrival of the railways into Ireland from the 1830s heralded one of the most drastic, albeit often beautiful, human-made changes to the Irish landscape. Bridges, viaducts, embankments and tunnels made their appearances across the length and breadth of the land. This humble bridge at Malahide, adjacent to the impressive estuary viaduct, carries the Dublin to Belfast line which was first inaugurated as the Dublin and Drogheda Railway in 1844.

Railway Cottages, Ballsbridge *(2000)*

Medium:	*Line & Watercolour*
Size:	*146mm (Wide) x 127mm (High)*
Reference No:	*WC015*

Railway Cottages, Ballsbridge: This charming line of twelve cottages, straddling the railway line between Lansdowne Road and Serpentine Avenue, were built in the 19th century for the railway workers attached to the Dublin to Kingstown (Dún Laoghaire) Railway Company.

The Temple Bar: *There are over 800 bars and taverns in Dublin and many of them date from the 19th century with classic Victorian interiors of carved wood, brass embellishments and atmospheric recesses. One such pub is 'The Temple Bar' situated at the corner of the streets known as Temple Bar (Temple Bar is also the name for the district) and Temple Lane South. It was founded in 1840, just a few years before the Great Famine decimated the population of Ireland. The pub is divided into a number of sections each with its own personality but all, including recent extensions, redolent of the best in traditional Irish pub interiors. Musicians play here daily both in impromptu and for scheduled sessions. Temple Bar, once the heartland of 18th and early 19th century Dublin docklands, was named after Sir William Temple, a 17th century landowner who held property in the area. Both streets were laid down in the 1660s.*

The Temple Bar (2003)	
Medium:	*Pen & Ink on Board*
Size:	*347mm (Wide) x 272mm (High)*
Reference No:	*DR016*

Rocque Map of Dublin, 1765

(Map in full colour on following pages)

Rocque Map 1765 (following pages): *John Rocque, a Huguenot map-maker from London, already famous for his maps of London, Paris and Rome, set up business in Dublin around 1754. Within four or five years he had produced a number of maps of Dublin including his 'Exact survey of the city and suburbs of Dublin' (1756) and also ones dealing with Dublin Bay and the whole county of Dublin. The version shown here was printed in 1767 with the title; 'Plan of the City and Suburbs of Dublin by J. Rocque Reduced from his large Plan'. His work, especially the maps executed in the larger scales, has been immensely useful to historians. The 1756 edition is of particular interest because it just predated the establishment of the Wide Streets Commission, a body which ultimately altered the face of the city from Parliament Street to Merrion Square.*

Rocque's street plans are relatively accurate, especially in his larger scale maps, as was proved recently when excavations were carried out on O'Connell Street Lower for a LUAS (light rail) electricity sub-station. His delineation for houses along this street, at a time when it was much narrower, was found to be quite precise when archaeologists discovered the old foundations. He calculated that based on the number of houses included on his large-scale maps the population of Dublin was 96,480, a figure now understood to be insufficient; it may have been closer to 150,000.

In this view it is obvious that the city had a well consolidated core and has moved considerably eastwards from the old medieval quarter. The newer or Georgian part of the city housed the wealthier classes while the poor generally remained behind in the older precincts which became more and more dilapidated. This latter situation created social and landscape problems right into recent times which are now only being comprehensively remedied. One of the features of Rocque's maps is the expression of his quite considerable illustrative and decorative skills which are only hinted at in this example.

Rocque Map *(2003)* - Next Page	
Medium:	*Line & Watercolour*
Size:	*557mm (Wide) x 377mm (High)*
Reference No:	*WC016*

REFERENCES ~
Churches

A · S.ᵗ Pauls
B · S.ᵗ Michans
C · S.ᵗ Marys
D · S.ᵗ Georges
E · S.ᵗ Thomass
F · S.ᵗ Jamess
G · S.ᵗ Catharines
H · S.ᵗ Audens
I · S.ᵗ Lukes
K · S.ᵗ Michaels
L · S.ᵗ Nicholas Within
M · Do Without
N · S.ᵗ Johns
O · S.ᵗ Werburghs
P · S.ᵗ Bridgets
Q · S.ᵗ Peters
R · S.ᵗ Kevans
S · S.ᵗ Andrews
T · S.ᵗ Anns
T · S.ᵗ Marks
U · Christ Church Cathedral
X · S.ᵗ Patricks Do
F.C · French Churches
P.M · Presbyterian Meeting Houses
Q.M · Quakers Do
M.M · Methodist Do
M.N · Moravion Do
A.B · Anna Babtist Do
✝ · Roman Chappels
G.H · Glass Houses
A · Bloody Bridge
B · Bridewell Do
C · Old Do
D · Ormond Do
E · Essex Do
1 · Carpenters Widows
2 · Grange gorman H
3 · Blue coat Hospital
4 · Linnen Hall
5 · Flax Manafactory
6 · Inns Q Infirmary
7 · Ormond Market
8 · Widows House
9 · Parish Schools
10 · Velvet Manafactory
11 · China Do
12 · Doct. Stevens Hospital
13 · St Patricks Do
14 · Work House
15 · Granary
16 · Soldiers Infirmary
17 · Court House
18 · Widows Do
19 · Black Dog
20 · New Gate
21 · Tholsel
22 · Musick Hall
23 · Four Courts
24 · Nicholas Hospit.ˡ
25 · Meath Do
26 · Mercers Do
27 · Incurables Do
28 · Poundens Foundery
D.C · Dutch Church
T.R · Theatre Royal
O.T · Old Do
N.T · New Do
29 · Provosts House

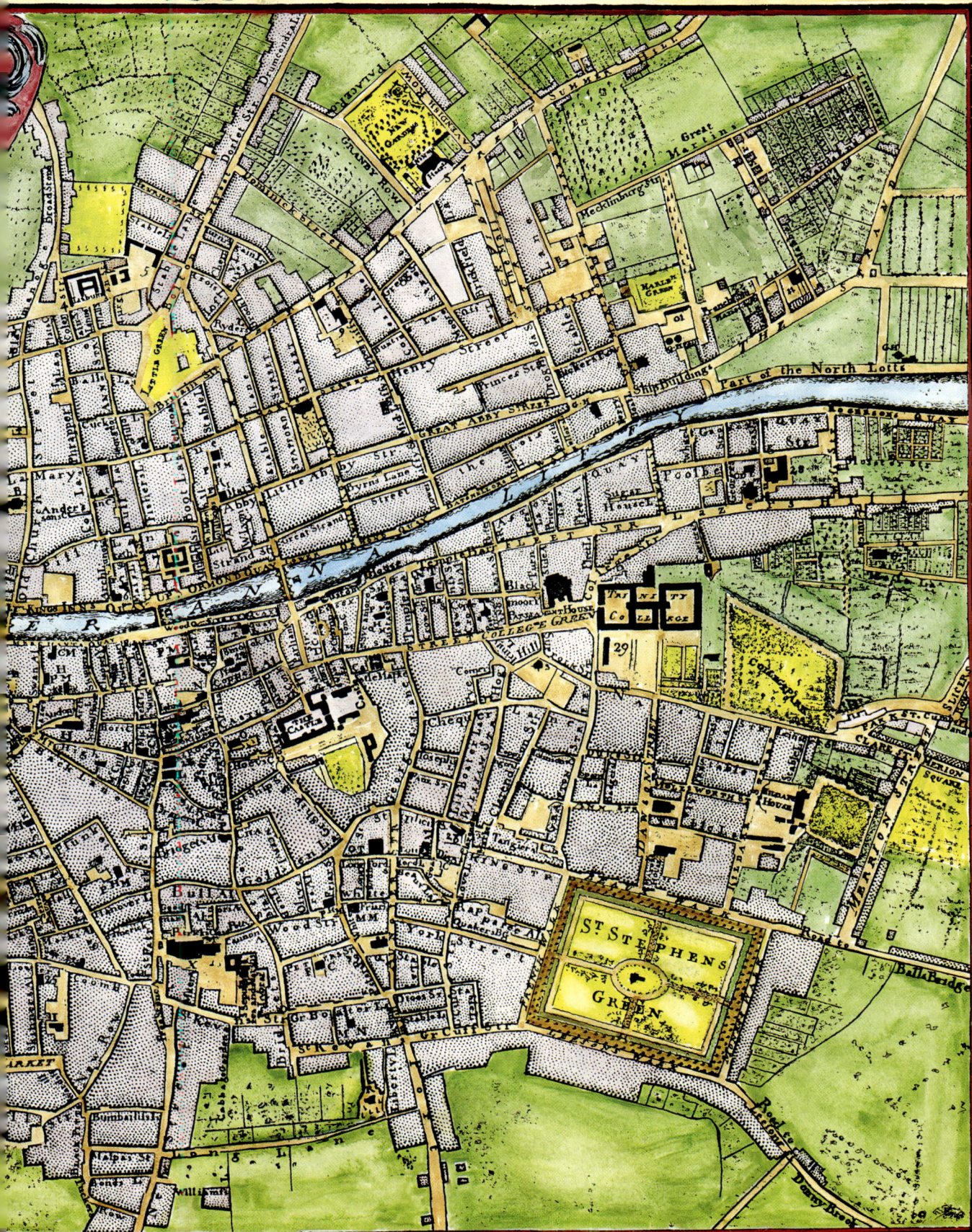

of Dublin By J. Rocque Reduc'd from his large PLAN

at the Bible in Castle Street & I. WILLIAMS *Skinner.*

P. Halpin *Sculps.*

Bank of Ireland, College Green: *The secret of longevity for a building has as much to do with its continued relevant usage as to the quality of its construction and such is the case with the Bank of Ireland on College Green. Since 1661 the Irish Parliament had been meeting in Chichester House, on College Green, but the accommodation there was both inadequate and in decay. A decision was made in 1727 to demolish Chichester House and to build a new Parliament House. Sir Edward Lovett Pearce was selected as the architect for what was to become the world's first building designed as a two-chamber legislature. The foundation stone was laid in 1728 and the work was substantially finished by 1733, the year Pearce died. The House of Commons occupied the centre of the arrangement under a Pantheon-style dome. A public gallery could and often did accommodate up to 700 spectators. The House of Lords was much smaller but no less elegant. The first session of Parliament took place in its new quarters in 1731 and its last was held in 1800 when the infamous Act of Union with Great Britain was ratified. The Bank of Ireland became the new owners of the redundant Parliament building in 1803. A stipulation of the sale required that all evidence of the building's former use was to be removed so the House of Commons disappeared but, thankfully, the House of Lords was surreptitiously saved preserving for posterity the most unique chamber of its kind to be found anywhere. Today this room probably represents the oldest intact legislative chamber in its original 18th century form in the world. The two tapestries, first hung in 1733, represent the Valiant Defence of Londonderry and the Glorious Battle of the Boyne. Their designer was Johann van der Hagen and the weaver was John van Beaver, Dutch craftsmen then living in Dublin. The fireplace surround was carved in oak by Thomas Oldham in 1748. The chandelier dates from 1788 and consists of 1,233 separate pieces of glass. It was made by Chebsey's Glass Works near Ballybough Bridge. Anyone can visit the House of Lords, and indeed the other public areas of this historic building, during normal banking hours.*

Bank of Ireland, College Green (2003)	
Medium:	*Pen & Ink on Board*
Size:	*310mm (Wide) x 195mm (High)*
Reference No:	*DR100*

Ranelagh Bridge, Royal Canal: *The Royal Canal, built between 1790 and 1817, was set up as a rival to the successful Grand Canal which had served the south side of the city since 1759. Unfortunately there was not enough business generated for the two canals and even though the Royal struggled on for well over a century it was finally closed to commercial traffic in 1961. That it survived at all was due to its purchase in 1845 by the Midland Great Western Railway Company so that a railway line could be built alongside the waterway. The canal, stretching from Spencer Dock on Dublin's North Wall to the River Shannon, is now being restored as a leisure amenity. Many of the old stone bridges have since become redundant with the building of new road crossings, a fate that befell Ranelagh Bridge in recent years when Dunsink Lane was carried across on a new span. Happily, this and other unused bridges are being preserved as memorials to the past and as picturesque features on the watery landscape.*

Ranelagh Bridge, Royal Canal (2000)	
Medium:	*Watercolour on Paper*
Size:	*182mm (Wide) x 195mm (High)*
Reference No:	*WC029*

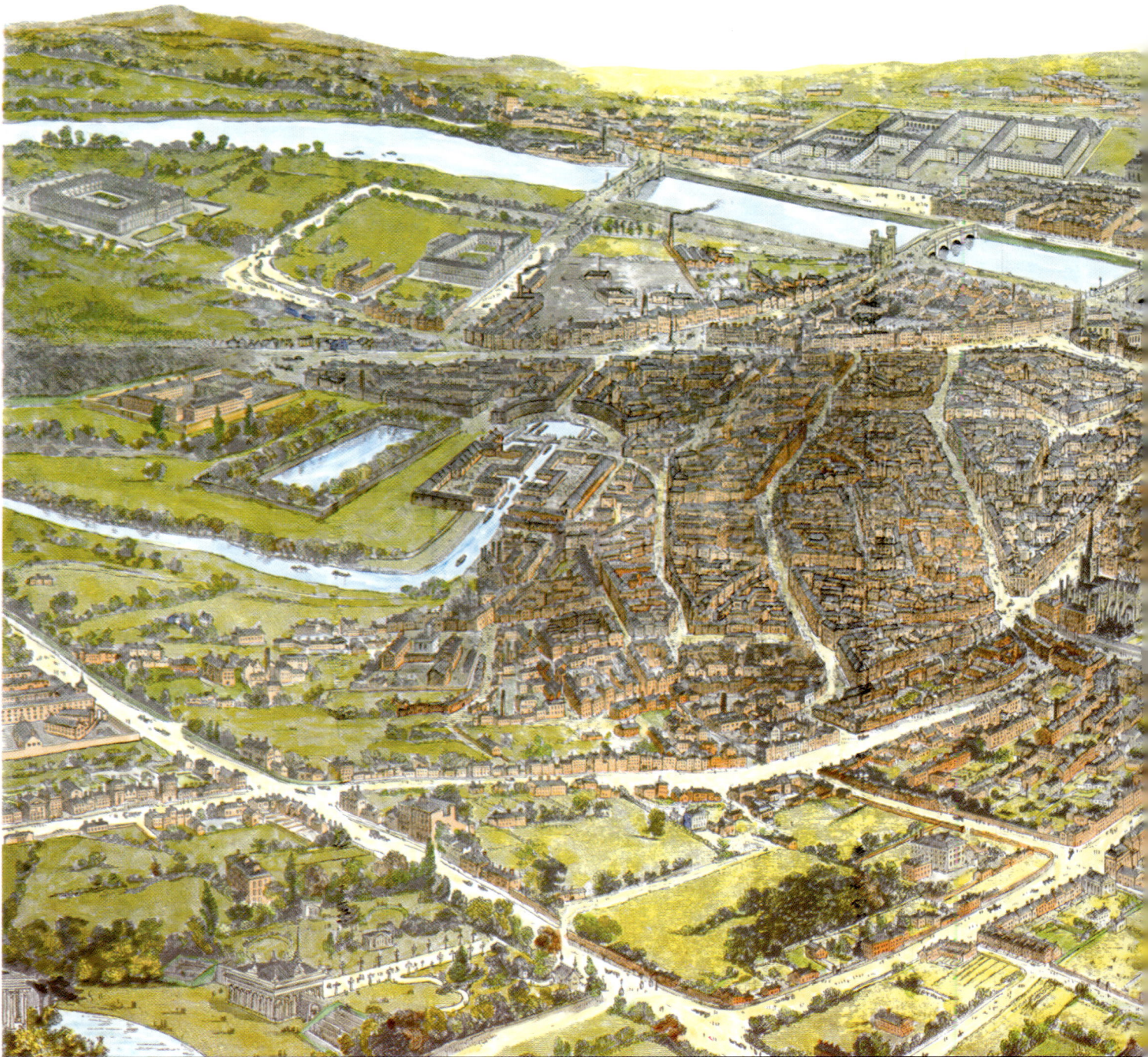

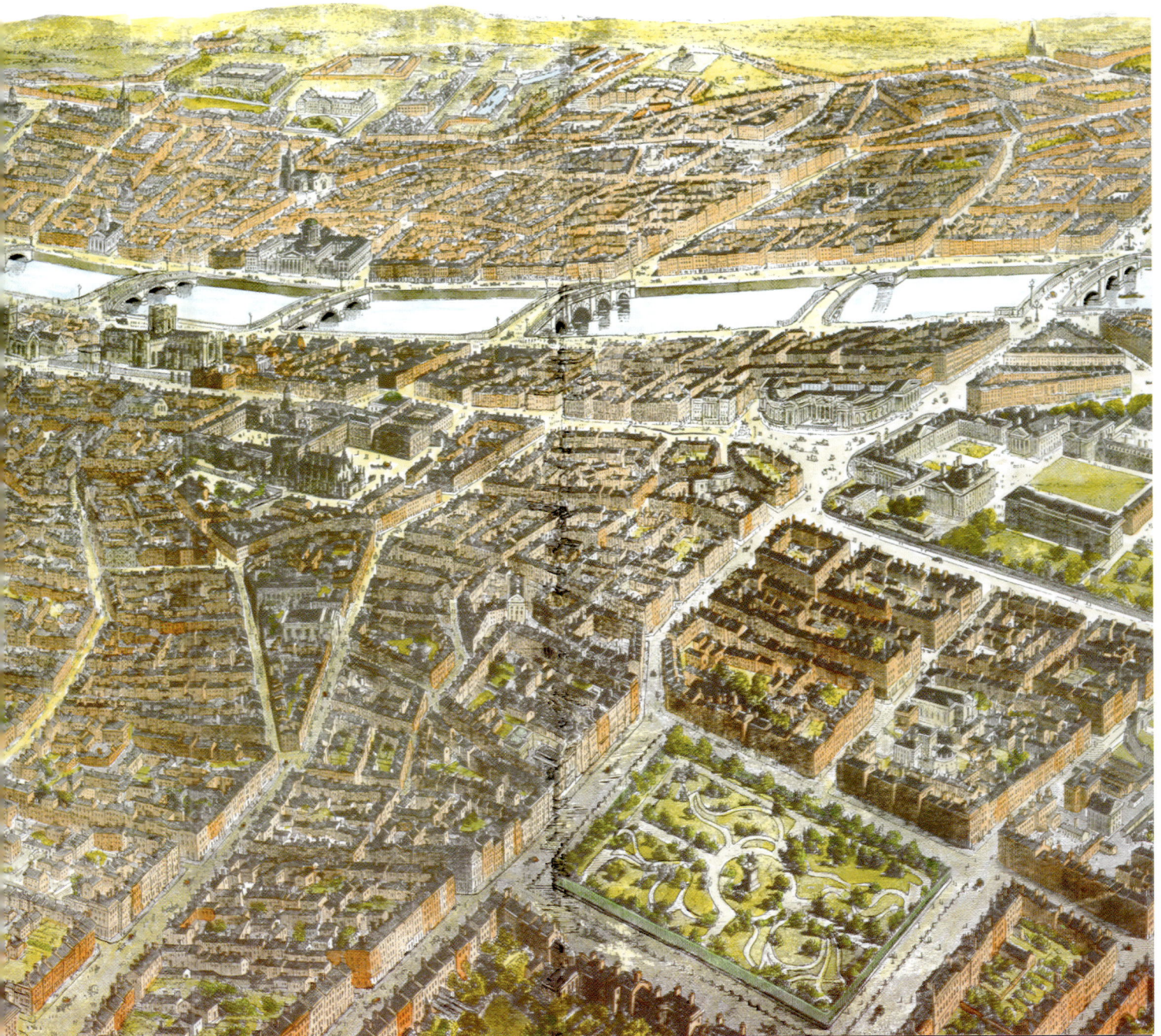

Bird's Eye View of Dublin, 1846

(Map in full colour on previous pages)

Bird's Eye View of Dublin, 1846 (previous pages): *In this 1846 bird's eye view of Dublin, published by the 'London Illustrated News' as the number one (no less!) in a series on the principal capitals of Europe, Dublin is represented as a prosperous and bustling city. The streets are full of life and commercial activity. Carriages and large numbers of pedestrians jostle along every roadway. The tight street patterns of the early town are still evident while the ordered splendour of the Georgian squares and boulevards are highlighted on the right-hand side of the drawing.*

By this time there were eight bridges spanning the River Liffey including the Wellington (Ha'penny) Bridge, built thirty years earlier, and the most easterly crossing, Carlisle (now the much-widened O'Connell) Bridge. All harbour activity has moved downstream of Carlisle Bridge. The wharves are choked with shipping as are the sheltered docks around the Custom House and in the Grand Canal Docks. A few of the ships are powered by steam engines and paddle wheels. Barges ply the Grand Canal and its spur into the harbour serving the Guinness Brewery. The two recently constructed railway lines (Dublin to Kingstown, 1836 and Dublin to Drogheda, 1844) march confidently across the south-eastern and north-eastern landscapes.

St Stephen's Green is still a railed-off private park. The equestrian statue by John Nost to George ll stands in the centre of the park. The large expanse of Trinity College offers a tranquil escape from the hurly-burly outside. Private mansions and institutions, several laid out with magnificent formal gardens, are dotted around the perimeter of the city. The main street, Sackville (now O'Connell) Street is still lined by Georgian terraces and dominated by the General Post Office and Nelson's Pillar.

In a sense, this representation gives a lie to the notion that the prosperity and significance of Dublin seriously declined after the 1800 Act of Union but then this drawing does not tell the whole story. While most of the streets exude an air of solidity and affluence the true situation was that a large proportion of the population lived in great poverty inside squalid tenements. There was a new trend, encouraged by the presence of the emerging railways, for the upper and merchant classes to move into the expanding suburbs while renting out their former city homes to the less-well off. To increase rental income from an impoverished clientele many unscrupulous landlords packed more and more families into single houses. Epidemics and diseases followed overcrowding and lack of sanitation. All this was only a prelude to the disasters that nearly overwhelmed the authorities when the effects of the Great Potato Famine, which had already begun in the countryside by 1846, spilled over into the capital itself.

Bird's Eye View of Dublin, 1846 *(2003)* - Previous Pages	
Medium:	*Watercolour on Board*
Size:	*932mm (Wide) x 300mm (High)*
Reference No:	*PR012*

Dublin, 1999

(Map in full colour on next page)

Dublin, 1999 (next page): *This map was the first prototype of the successful series of tourist maps, 'The Dublin Visitor Map & Guide', which was launched in 1999. In the event the particular design shown here was modified before the first in the series was printed. Designed by this author and published by DMCRS Ltd, a subsidiary of the Dublin City Business Association (DCBA), the 'Dublin Visitor Map & Guide' has been an outstanding success in its objectives. Up to 1999 there had been no free detailed map available for visitors to the city and this publication filled that gap. Since its inception over one million copies of the map and guide are printed and distributed on the home market annually. Unusually for a map of this sort the content is completely updated each year to reflect the rapidly changing city. This means that no fewer than one hundred amendments are incorporated into each new edition. From an historian's point of view, he or she can chart the changing landscape of Dublin by comparing one year with the next. An important feature of the map is the inclusion of colour coding to highlight the individual districts of the city such as the Shopping, Georgian, Medieval, Dockland and Temple Bar districts. The latest edition, year 2003, is discussed and shown on pages 57 – 59. Incidentally, the 2004 edition will have to have major adjustments carried out to accommodate the new Luas (light rail) lines.*

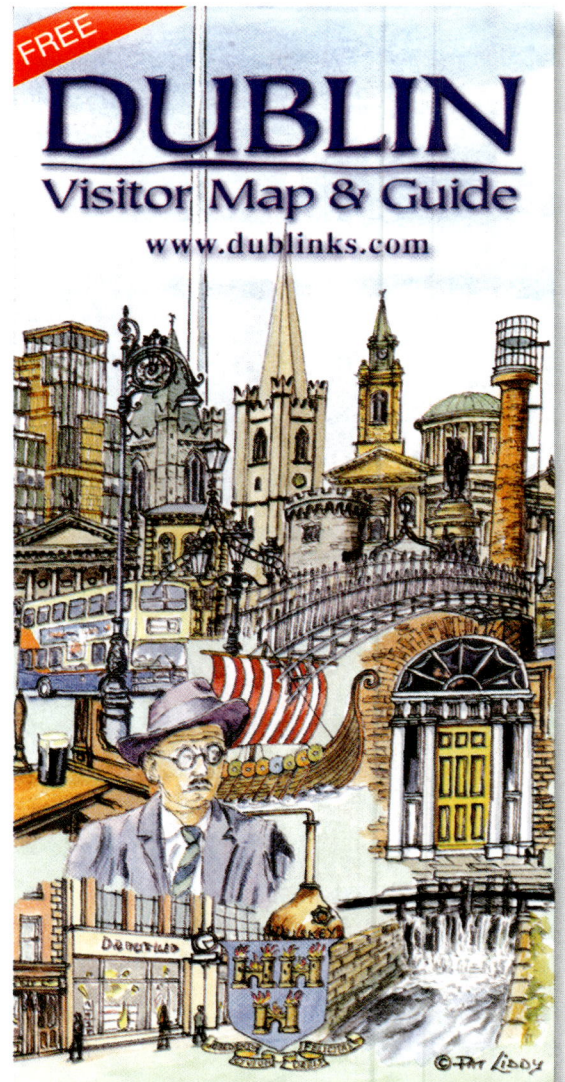

Dublin Visitor Map & Guide 2003: *The cover of the 2003 edition of the 'Dublin Visitor Map & Guide'.*

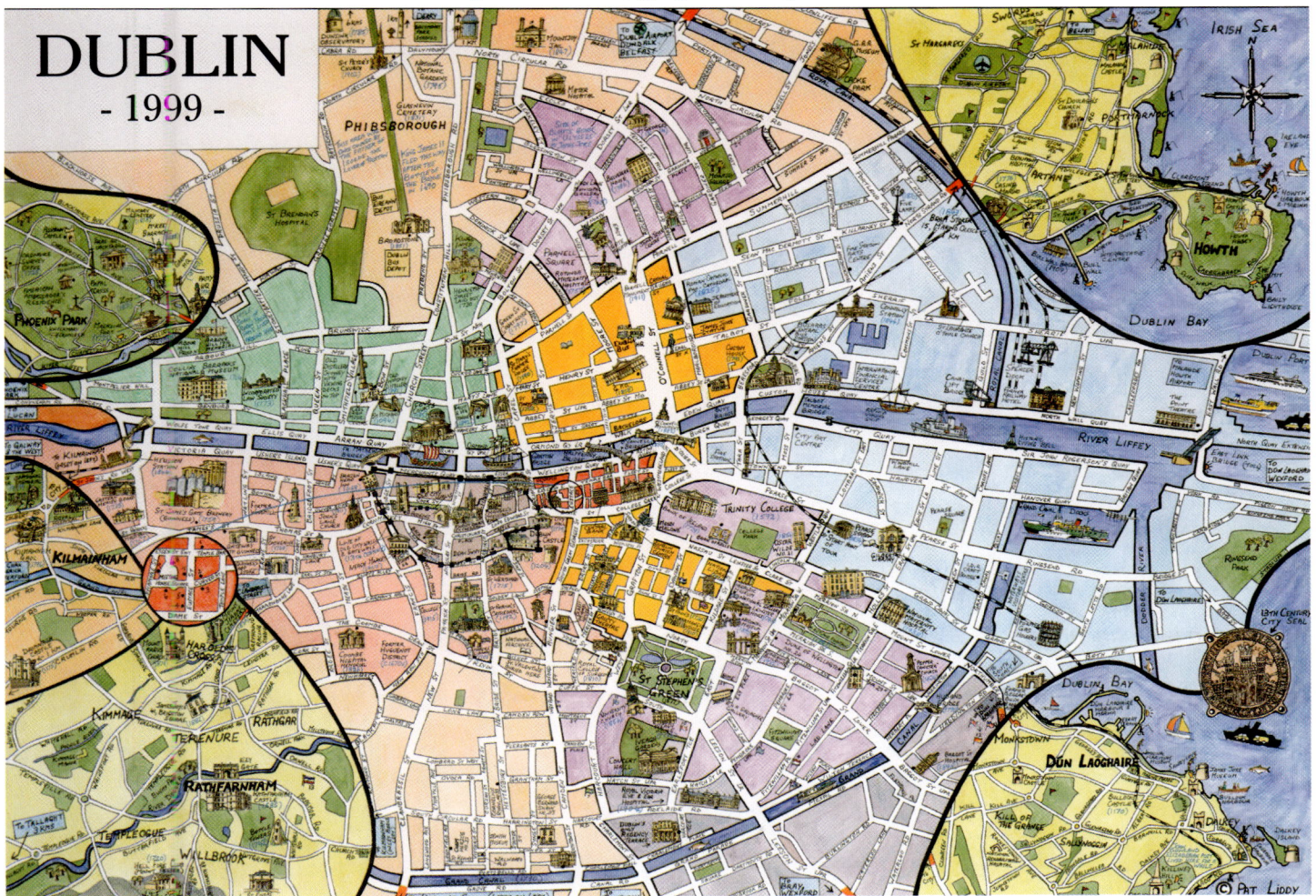

DUBLIN
- 1999 -

Dublin Visitor Map & Guide - Original Prototype (1999)

Medium:	Watercolour on Paper
Size:	730mm (Wide) x 525mm (High)
Reference No:	WC105

Ireland's Eye: Standing like a sentinel at the northern approach to Dublin Bay, Ireland's Eye has seen the human comings and goings for thousands of years, from prehistoric voyagers to pillaging Vikings, from fishing boats to gigantic super-ferries. While Dublin and its shores have changed immeasurably over the last two thousand years the island itself has hardly altered a jot. A ruined early Christian church, a couple of stony pathways going nowhere and a forlorn and empty Martello tower, built to thwart a possible invasion by Napoleon, are the only traces of human interference. Today the island is home only to thousands of seabirds. Ireland's Eye ('Ey' was Norse for 'island') has been a witness, perhaps even a jaundiced spectator, to the not always harmonious efforts of the mainlanders to progress their notions of civilisation.

Ireland's Eye (2002)	
Medium:	*Watercolour on Paper*
Size:	*495mm (Wide) x 365mm (High)*
Reference No:	*WC017*

Map of Dublin, 2003
(Map in full colour on following pages)

Map of Dublin 2003 (following pages): *This map is the latest in the series of the free publication 'The Dublin Visitor Map & Guide' (see page 54). The progress of change in the city over the previous year or two is charted on the map and includes;*

- *New boardwalks along the north quays of the River Liffey.*
- *Additional bridges across the Liffey including the Millennium Bridge and the James Joyce Bridge. Two planned new bridges are also indicated.*
- *The growing number of pedestrian routes are shown (in orange) but more routes are likely over the next few years.*
- *The regeneration of the redundant and neglected old port area on either side of the Liffey's quays, on a scale never before seen in Ireland, into the vibrant new office, apartment and cultural areas of the north side and southside Docklands.*
- *New visitor centres such as the Chester Beatty Library Galleries, The Guinness Storehouse, the Smithfield Chimney and the GAA Museum. Next year will see the addition of the 'Dracula' Museum – the author of, reputedly, the world's best-selling novel, Bram Stoker, was born at Marino on Dublin's north side.*
- *New monuments such as 'The Spire' and 'The Linesman'.*
- *New public squares including St. Mary's and Grand Canal Square.*
- *The line of the new Port Tunnel. Next year's map will show the lines of the new light rail system, the Luas.*

The map also shows the extensiveness and quality of the tourist 'product' available throughout the city centre core, on both sides of the river. A generation ago it was felt that all Dublin had to offer the visitor was Trinity College, Dublin Castle, the two cathedrals, a Georgian square or two and a shabby downtown area. Today, there are dozens of world-class museums, galleries, visitor centres, heritage sites and scenic spots to be enjoyed by both citizen and visitor. The distinctive cityscape has been largely cleaned, shopping precincts are on a par with any city and the emerging developments are creating new and exciting quarters.

Map of Dublin 2003 *(2003)* - Next Page

Medium:	*Laminated Print*
Size:	*1,372mm (Wide) x 926mm (High)*
Reference No:	*PR011*

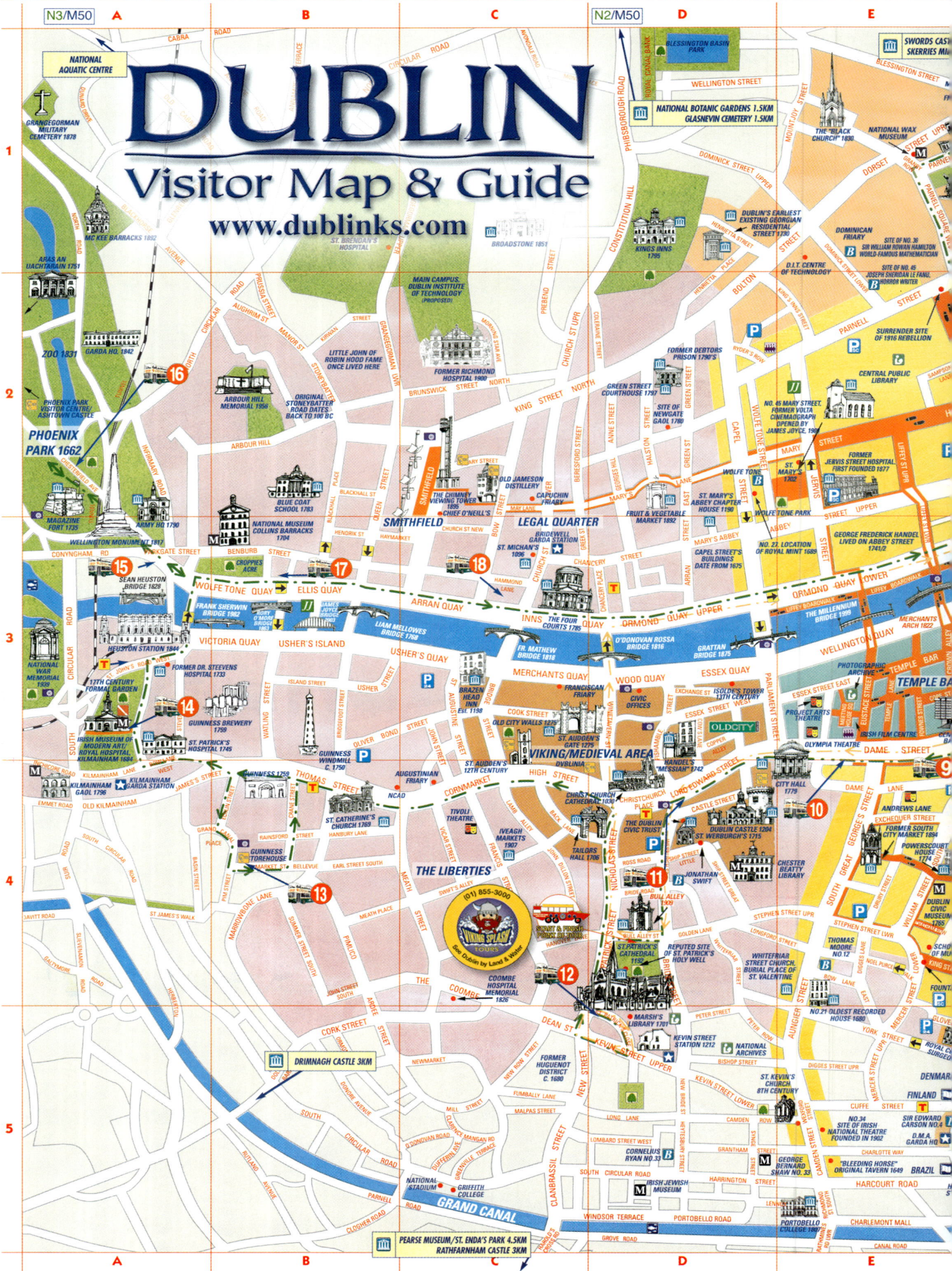

DUBLIN
Visitor Map & Guide
www.dublinks.com

National Aquatic Centre

Grangegorman Military Cemetery 1878

Áras an Uachtaráin 1751

Zoo 1831

Phoenix Park Visitor Centre/Ashtown Castle

PHOENIX PARK 1662

Magazine Fort 1735

Wellington Monument 1817

National War Memorial 1939

17th Century Formal Garden

Irish Museum of Modern Art/ Royal Hospital Kilmainham 1684

Kilmainham Gaol 1796

Kilmainham Garda Station

MC KEE BARRACKS 1892

GARDA HQ 1942

Arbour Hill Memorial 1956

Blue Coat School 1783

National Museum Collins Barracks 1704

Croppies Acre

Sean Heuston Bridge 1828

Frank Sherwin Bridge 1982

Rory O'More Bridge 1861

James Joyce Bridge 2003

Liam Mellowes Bridge 1768

Heuston Station 1844

Guinness Brewery 1759

Guinness Windmill c. 1750

St. Patrick's Hospital 1745

Guinness Storehouse

St. Catherine's Church 1769

NCAD

Augustinian Friary

THE LIBERTIES

Coombe Hospital Memorial 1826

Drimnagh Castle 3km

National Stadium

Griffith College

GRAND CANAL

Pearse Museum/St. Enda's Park 4.5km Rathfarnham Castle 3km

St. Brendan's Hospital

Broadstone 1851

Main Campus, Dublin Institute of Technology (proposed)

Former Richmond Hospital 1900

Little John of Robin Hood fame once lived here

Original Stoneybatter road dates back to 100 BC

Kings Inns 1795

SMITHFIELD

The Chimney Viewing Tower 1895

Chief O'Neill's

Old Jameson Distillery

Capuchin Friary

LEGAL QUARTER

Green Street Courthouse 1797

Site of Newgate Gaol 1780

Fruit & Vegetable Market 1892

St. Michan's 1096

Bridewell Garda Station

Wolfe Tone Park

St. Mary's Abbey Chapter House 1190

Capel Street's Buildings date from 1675

No. 27, Location of Royal Mint 1689

The Four Courts 1785

INNS QUAY

Fr. Mathew Bridge 1818

O'Donovan Rossa Bridge 1816

Grattan Bridge 1875

ORMOND QUAY UPPER

WELLINGTON QUAY

The Millennium Bridge 1999

Liffey Boardwalk

MERCHANTS QUAY

Franciscan Friary

WOOD QUAY

Isolde's Tower 13th Century

Civic Offices

ESSEX QUAY

Exchange St

Old City Walls 1275

St. Audeon's Gate 1275

VIKING/MEDIEVAL AREA

DUBHLINN

St. Audeon's 12th Century

Handel's "Messiah" 1742

Christ Church Cathedral 1030

The Dublin Civic Trust

Dublin Castle 1204

St. Werburgh's 1715

City Hall 1779

Chester Beatty Library

Jonathan Swift

Tivoli Theatre

Iveagh Markets 1907

Tailors Hall 1706

St. Patrick's Cathedral

Reputed site of St. Patrick's Holy Well

Marsh's Library 1701

Kevin Street Station 1212

National Archives

St. Kevin's Church 8th Century

Whitefriar Street Church, Burial Place of St. Valentine

No. 21 Oldest Recorded House 1660

Thomas Moore No. 12

Powerscourt House 1774

Former South City Market 1894

Dublin Civic Museum

National Theatre founded in 1902

George Bernard Shaw No. 33

"Bleeding Horse" Original Tavern 1649

Irish Jewish Museum

Portobello College 1807

National Botanic Gardens 1.5km Glasnevin Cemetery 1.5km

Blessington Basin Park

Wellington Street

The "Black Church" 1830

National Wax Museum

Dublin's earliest existing Georgian residential street 1730

Dominican Friary

Site of No. 36 Sir William Rowan Hamilton World-famous Mathematician

Site of No. 45 Joseph Sheridan Le Fanu horror writer

D.I.T. Centre of Technology

Central Public Library

Surrender site of 1916 Rebellion

No. 45 Mary Street, Former Volta Cinematograph opened by James Joyce 1909

Former Debtors Prison 1790's

Former Jervis Street Hospital first founded 1877

George Frederick Handel lived on Abbey Street 1741/2

TEMPLE BAR

Photographic Archive

Project Arts Theatre

Irish Film Centre

Olympia Theatre

Merchants Arch 1822

Swords Castle Skerries Mills

(01) 855-3000 VIKING SPLASH TOURS — See Dublin by Land & Water

Map of Dublin

North Georgian Area

North Docklands Area

International Financial Services Centre (IFSC)

South Docklands Area

Trinity College 1592

Merrion Square 1752

South Georgian Area

St. Stephen's Green 1663

Iveagh Gardens 1865

Fairview Park

Royal Canal 1790

River Liffey

Grand Canal 1791

Custom House 1791

The General Post Office 1818

The Spire of Dublin

Dublin Bus Head Office

City Seal 13th Century

Not to exact scale. © Pat Liddy

O'Connell Street: *Until around four centuries ago the site of O'Connell Street, Dublin's principal boulevard, stood on what was the open sea of the River Liffey estuary (see map on pages 6/7). At low tide one could walk across the exposed sloblands but until the reclamations of the late 17th century the high tide completely covered the area. When development did take place the present upper part of O'Connell Street was initially laid down with a narrow street called Drogheda Street. This street continued by means of a cramped lane down to the river front. In the 1750s a great developer of his day, Luke Gardiner, took over ownership of lands that included Drogheda Street. He broadened the street to its present width and lined his new avenue with Georgian terraces and mansions. The centre of the street, by now called Sackville Street, was dedicated to a gravel mall, complete with a fountain, on which the gentry promenaded. As a result of the destruction caused by the 1916 Rising and the Civil War of 1922/3 only one of these period houses survives; number 40, now part of the Royal Dublin Hotel. In 1795 the new Carlisle (now O'Connell) Bridge was opened, by which time the widened street was extended to the river. John Henry Foley designed the memorial to Daniel O'Connell which was unveiled to admiring crowds gathered in the pouring rain on 15th August 1882. O'Connell, known as the Liberator, had achieved religious freedom in Ireland through the 1829 Act of Emancipation. His further efforts to have the Act of Union rescinded met with no success and he died on his way to Rome in 1847. The Spire, completed in 2003, stands on the spot where once stood Nelson Pillar. Erected in 1808 to the memory of Admiral Horatio Nelson, the victor of Trafalgar, the column was blown up in 1966. Its 120m stainless steel replacement was designed by Ian Ritchie, a London-based architect. The principal classical building on O'Connell Street is the General Post Office built in 1814-18 to a design by Francis Johnston.*

O'Connell Street (2003)

Medium:	*Pen & Ink on Board*
Size:	*246mm (Wide) x 286mm (High)*
Reference No:	*DR017*

Dublin in the Year 2050

(Map in full colour on following pages)

What the future holds for Dublin, even for informed commentators, is anybody's guess. So many factors imported or forced upon Ireland from the world at large may accelerate, deflect or even shatter the normal evolutionary dynamics at play in the city and within the country itself.

Cities can become fraught places to live and work in. Many people in Dublin are at their wits' end trying to cope with ever-lengthening commuting journeys, traffic delays, inadequate public transport, severe time pressures, the cost of housing and education, a stretched health service and a rise in crime, among other issues. According to the forecasters of a mere twenty years ago, by now we were supposed to be a paperless society with endless leisure opportunities. Instead we are swamped with paper and bureaucracy and have to constantly reshuffle our lives against a grave shortage of that precious commodity; time.

An improved Dublin will be a city where a fully integrated transport system comprising mainline rail, light rail, a metro system and a truly comprehensive bus service will leave nobody further than a ten minute walk from the nearest public transport. The spiralling outward growth of the city will have been curtailed within a defined region where an increasingly concentrated population (of over 2 million) can justify and make more economical a highly developed infrastructure including roads, housing, schools, hospitals as well as the enhanced public transport as aforementioned. City living will benefit from a greater harmony between work and commuting time as well as from new or expanded cultural centres and neighbourhood cores, better developed green and waterway areas, the elimination of deprived districts and a reduction in crime.

Further pain will have to be felt to achieve these goals. For example, the Port Tunnel, the subject of much negative debate generally and especially from residents living above or close to its construction sites, will only be the first of several more (albeit shorter ones) if traffic is to be relieved from the streets of the city centre. Luas will have to be expanded within the city centre and inner suburbs. Light rail (i.e. Luas) should not be confused with heavy rail (Metro/DART). The former is essentially designed for moving people relatively short distances with frequent, convenient stops. Metro is the way forward for speedily transporting significant numbers of people to and from the city centre and between the outer suburbs.

There is probably no such thing as an ideal city but the collected wisdom that is now available, both from our own hard-won experiences and that gained from other countries, should bring us closer to a smoother-running, more liveable-in and less frustrating Dublin. Those same experiences, however, should also caution citizens to be constantly on guard to ensure that common sense and vision are not filtered and distorted through the prism of political expediency.

On page 64 is a list of some positive features of change that should take place in the city by the middle of this century, at least as this writer sees them. For a myriad of reasons they may not happen before 2050 or some, indeed, may never come to pass at all. Many of us will not be around to find out but this generation of decision-makers must plant the acorns.

Dublin in the Year 2050 *(2003)* - Next Page	
Medium:	*Line & Watercolour*
Size:	*720mm (Wide) x 510mm (High)*
Reference No:	*WC106*

2050

The Growth of Dublin

Medieval
C.1720
C.1820
outlining continuous high- & medium density areas

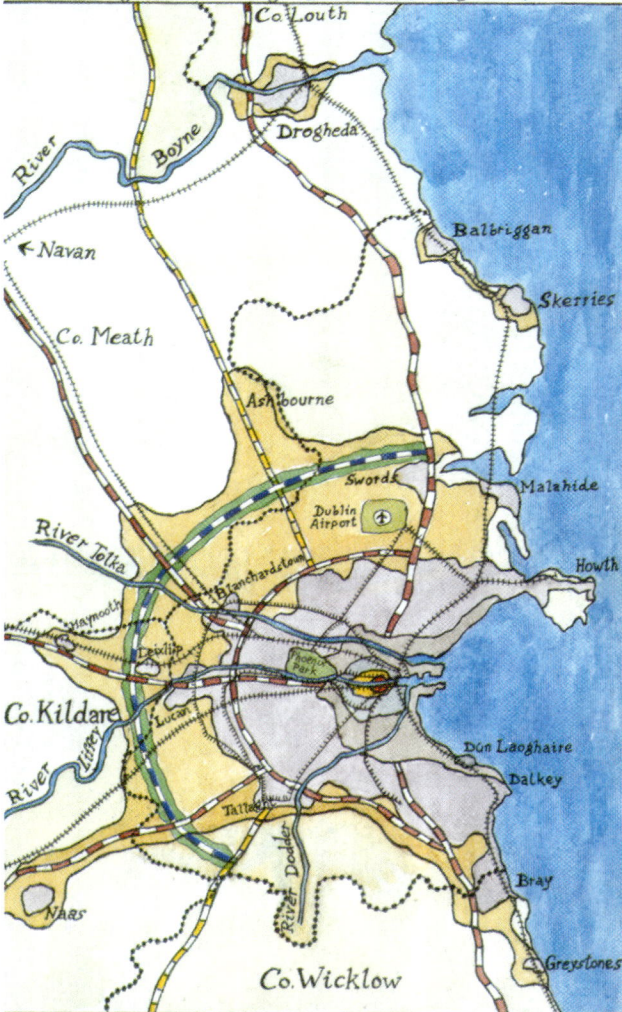

C. 1900
2000
2050

Co. Louth
Drogheda
← Navan
Co. Meath
Balbriggan
Skerries
Ashbourne
Swords
Dublin Airport
Malahide
Blanchardstown
Howth
River Tolka
Maynooth
Lucan
Co. Kildare
Leixlip
Tallaght
Dun Laoghaire
Dalkey
River Liffey
River Dodder
Bray
Naas
Co. Wicklow
Greystones

Motorway with Woodland Greenbelt
Motorway
Dual Carriageway
County Boundary
Main Line Rail, Suburban Rail
Luas & Metro

New Bridges
Flood/Tidal Barriers
Boardwalk
New Pedestrian Route
Current Pedestrian Route
Metro Station-entrance
Road Tunnel-entrance

New Civic Squares
New Green Belts
Major Redevelopment (post 2'003)
Luas Light Rail
DART/Suburban Rail
Metro
Vehicle Tunnels

Villages of Dublin
Distinct districts throughout city & suburbs re-emerge with
• Individual identities
• Quality Environments
• Self-sufficient facilities

Grangegorman
Dublin's 4th University Campus including a new medical campus. Reopened Rail/Luas line heavily landscaped & area generally intensively landscaped and wooded

Markets Area
Former Wholesale Fruit & Vegetable Market transformed into vibrant retail market and residential area along new Pedestrian Route to Smithfield

Shoppi
Henry St, Mary St Talbot St & Abbey Consolidated int largest & most Shopping C Dawson St & Cla Pedestrianised & Grafton Stree Shopping Pre

Smithfield
Dublin's main Civic Space now a major attraction with
• significant sculptures/monuments
• pavement cafes
• vibrant street life
• performing events
• visitor attractions

The Digital Hub
Multi Media & I.T. Centre (former Guinness property) Other redundant industrial areas around city similarly transformed
(above: old Windmill at Digital Hub restored)

Heuston Gateway
Area around Heuston Station developed into a new mixed-use, high density Urban Centre (including some high-rise)

Liffey Quays
• Boardwalks along entire length
• Traffic Calming
• Widened Pedestrian Routes
• More Trees
• Water Taxi Stops

Metro
(Heavy Rai Underground w for rapid mass betwee City Centre & & Interconnec between Transp

Dublin Castle

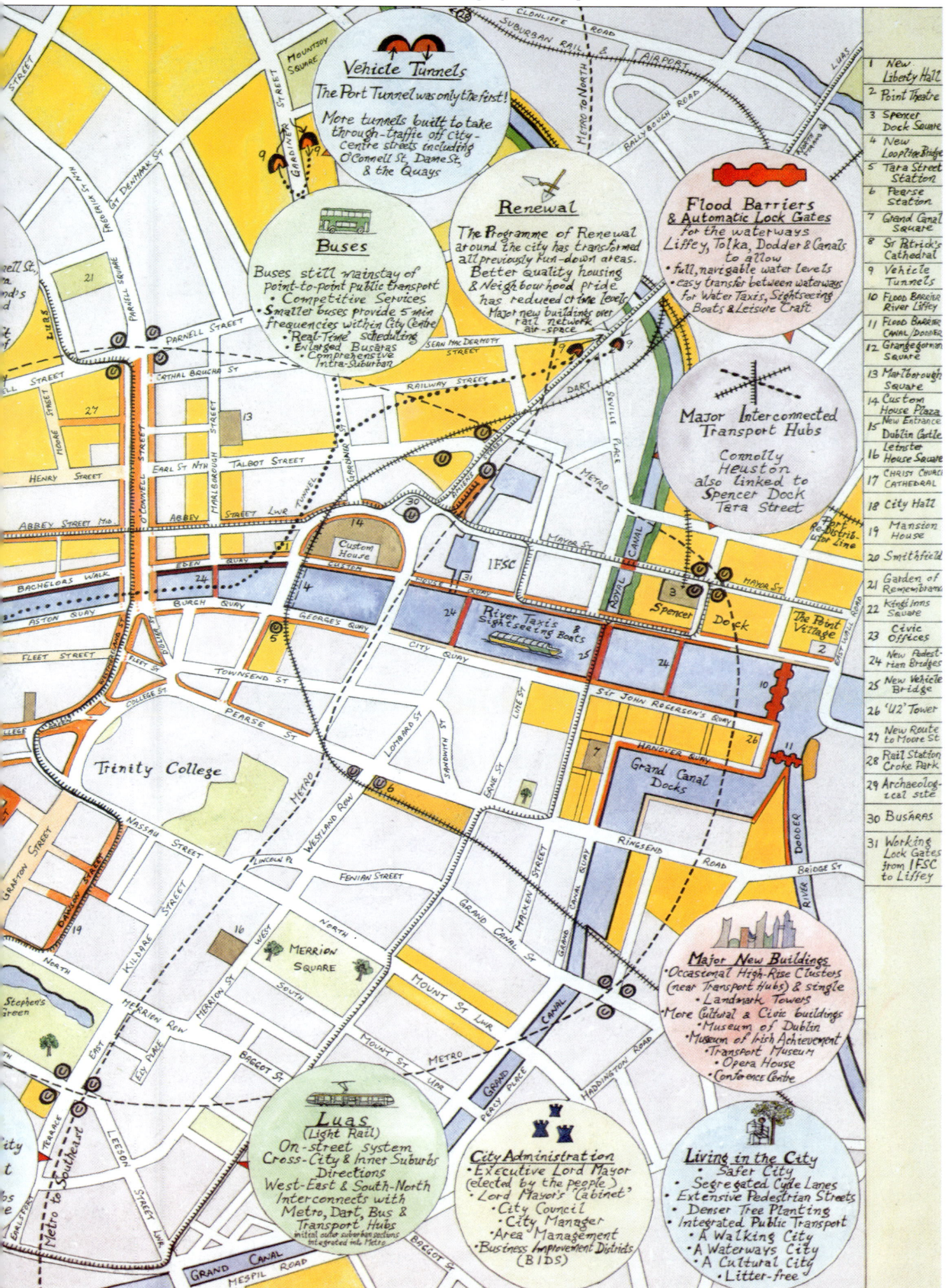

Vehicle Tunnels
The Port Tunnel was only the first!
More tunnels built to take through-traffic off city centre streets including O'Connell St, Dame St, & the Quays

Buses
Buses still mainstay of point-to-point public transport
• Competitive Services
• Smaller buses provide 5 min frequencies within City Centre
• 'Real-Time' scheduling
• Enlarged Busáras
• Comprehensive Intra-Suburban

Renewal
The Programme of Renewal around the city has transformed all previously run-down areas. Better quality housing & Neighbourhood pride has reduced crime levels. Major new buildings over rail network air-space.

Flood Barriers
& Automatic Lock Gates
for the waterways Liffey, Tolka, Dodder & Canals to allow
• full, navigable water levels
• easy transfer between waterways for Water Taxis, Sightseeing Boats & Leisure Craft

Major Interconnected Transport Hubs
Connolly Heuston also linked to Spencer Dock Tara Street

River Taxis & Sightseeing Boats

Major New Buildings
• Occasional High-Rise Clusters (near Transport Hubs) & single Landmark Towers
• More Cultural & Civic buildings
• Museum of Dublin
• Museum of Irish Achievement
• Transport Museum
• Opera House
• Conference Centre

Luas (Light Rail)
On-street system
Cross-City & Inner Suburbs Directions
West-East & South-North
Interconnects with Metro, Dart, Bus & Transport Hubs
initial outer suburban sections integrated into Metro

City Administration
• Executive Lord Mayor (elected by the people)
• Lord Mayor's 'Cabinet'
• City Council
• City Manager
• Area Management
• Business Improvement Districts (BIDs)

Living in the City
• Safer City
• Segregated Cycle Lanes
• Extensive Pedestrian Streets
• Denser Tree Planting
• Integrated Public Transport
• A Walking City
• A Waterways City
• A Cultural City
• Litter-free

Trinity College
Merrion Square
Stephen's Green
Grand Canal Docks
IFSC
Custom House
Spencer Dock
The Point Village

1	New Liberty Hall
2	Point Theatre
3	Spencer Dock Square
4	New Loopline Bridge
5	Tara Street Station
6	Pearse Station
7	Grand Canal Square
8	St Patrick's Cathedral
9	Vehicle Tunnels
10	Flood Barrier River Liffey
11	Flood Barrier Canal/Dodder
12	Grangegorman Square
13	Marlborough Square
14	Custom House Plaza New Entrance
15	Dublin Castle Leinster
16	House Square
17	Christ Church Cathedral
18	City Hall
19	Mansion House
20	Smithfield
21	Garden of Remembrance
22	King's Inns Square
23	Civic Offices
24	New Pedestrian Bridges
25	New Vehicle Bridge
26	'U2' Tower
27	New Route to Moore St
28	Rail Station Croke Park
29	Archaeological site
30	Busáras
31	Working Lock Gates from IFSC to Liffey

Dublin in the Year 2050
(Map in full colour on the previous pages)

Transport
- Major Transport Hubs (Connolly, Heuston, Tara Street, Spencer Dock) developed.
- 4 Luas lines in operation (from inner suburbs and within city centre).
- 4 Metro lines serving outer suburbs.
- A Metro interconnector between Transport Hubs.
- Safer dedicated Cycle Lanes.
- New outer ring motorway in green belt corridor.
- Improved public transport reducing car ownership.
- Dublin Port: Radical rebuilding and reorganisation. Rail from Dublin Port to Distribution Centres.
- Busáras largely underground - also serving Connolly Transport Hub.
- Cross-City Vehicle Tunnels.
- Rail station complex serving Croke Park.
- Loopline Railway Bridge rebuilt with a low-level parapet (to open view to Custom House).
- Electric Minibuses every 5/10 minutes serving non-Luas quadrants within city centre.
- Dublin Airport handling 50 million passengers per annum.

Waterways
- Boardwalks along length of Liffey Quays.
- Flood/Tidal Barriers on Liffey, Dodder & Tolka. Low-tide 'emptiness' solved.
- Automatic fast-filling Lock-Gates between rivers, canals and IFSC.
- Water Taxis and Sightseeing Boats on the above interconnected waterways.
- More bridges as necessary.

Major Renewal
- The enhanced Docklands Area home to 100,000 additional residents.
- Market District (former Fruit & Vegetable Market) and Smithfield successful Civic Areas.
- Development of Heuston Gateway (Heuston Station area).
- Grangegorman (site of future university campus, beside new rail/Luas lines).
- 'Air space' over mainline rails largely used for building.
- Reinforced local neighbourhoods ('Villages of Dublin') with an individual identity and a comprehensive supply of shops and facilities.
- Former Inner City 'ghettos' transformed into highly-desirable mixed-class neighbourhoods.
- All areas formerly dominated by low-grade or redundant buildings totally revamped.
- New Business Improvement Districts (BIDS) will empower local business communities to upgrade and maintain street standards locally.

The Built City
- High-rise (20/30 storeys) in clusters or single towers near Transport Hubs.
- Liberty Hall rebuilt.
- All heritage buildings restored and in full-time use.
- Higher density developments (e.g. Baldoyle, Lucan, North Fringe, Ashtown, Docklands) with self-sufficient town centres.
- High-density redevelopment finished moving eastwards in favour of westwards (Heuston, Inchicore, Ballyfermot etc).

Environment
- Significantly increased tree planting. Generally a greener city.
- Consistent Blue Flag beaches.
- On-street litter vastly reduced.
- Dedicated walks and cycle lanes around Coast.
- Canals restored & navigable.

City Living
- Family-friendly apartments and facilities.
- New Opera/Concert venue.
- Larger Abbey complex.
- Docklands Water Activities and Cultural Centres.
- Large Soccer cum Athletic Stadium.
- More public 'squares' in City Centre.
- Quays – wider footpaths & less traffic.
- Increased Pedestrian Streets and Routes.
- Reduction in Crime. More Garda presence.

Tourism
- Frequent Cruise Ships calls to Dublin Port.
- International Conference Centre.
- Large hotels near Port.
- More museums/activity centres including a Dublin Museum, an Irish Achievements Centre and a Transport (air/land/sea) Museum.
- Expanded tourist product (tourism has potential to at least treble by 2050).
- Dublin designated a 'Walking City'.
- Regenerated and safer streets.
- Permanent Archaeological Site and Visitor Centre around Cook Street.

Shopping
- Henry Street/O'Connell Street precinct country's largest Shopping Centre.
- Expansion of pedestrian zones around the Grafton Street area.
- Grafton Street partially glassed in. Smaller specialist shops abound in side streets.
- Luas and minibuses make travel easier between northside and southside shopping precincts.

Part 02
Changes in Motion

The transition of Dublin from a tiny Celtic village to a major world metropolis has not been without its traumas, setbacks, disasters and political hindrances. Nevertheless, the city did grow and sometimes prosper. With prosperity today being even more evident than at any time in the past, problems and pressures remain which effect the life-style and well-being of many people especially those thousands who feel left behind in the wake of the so-called Celtic Tiger (this aggressive feline has become more of a pussycat now that the economy has slowed down somewhat since 2002). If the living standards of the more vulnerable in society are being threatened by the cost-of-living in what has become one of Europe's most expensive cities, at least sub-standard housing is generally becoming a thing of the past. Many of the older generation public housing complexes are being demolished and replaced by buildings of more substance and character. There are immense developments under way and this part of the book looks at some of these schemes, some big, some small, that have just come on stream or are due to enhance the streetscapes and skyline of Dublin in the immediate future.

Rooftops *(1998)* - Next Page	
Medium:	*Oil on Canvas*
Size:	*595mm (Wide) x 885mm (High)*
Reference No:	*OL010*

The Rooftops of Dublin: *This view is taken over the rooftops of Dame Street looking towards the west. The towers and domes that project above the parapets of Dame Street include (from the left): Dublin Castle, St Michael's (Dublinia), City Hall, Christ Church Cathedral and John's Lane church.*

Tara Street Station: *The dramatic new office building and rail concourse which will rise above the rebuilt DART station on Tara Street.*

Tara Street Station and Tower (2003)

Medium:	*Line & Watercolour*
Size:	*570mm (Wide) x 440mm (High)*
Reference No:	*WC019*

Tara Street Station

The first railway to run in Ireland was the Dublin to Kingstown (Dún Laoghaire) line in 1834. The terminus for this operation was at Westland Row. Ten years later the terminus for the Dublin to Drogheda Railway was opened at Amiens Street. For years these two railways operated in splendid isolation until 1891 when the so-called Loop Line was erected over the city's streets to connect the two stations. Cutting through a number of buildings which inconveniently stood in the way before passing over the River Liffey, this extension skirted Tara Street before diagonally crossing Pearse Street and the grounds of Trinity College on its way to Westland Row. The building of the Loop Line afforded the opportunity of opening a minor station at Tara Street.

Up to a decade ago, Tara Street Station was officially not a station at all; it was only a halt and didn't even warrant a stationmaster of its own. All that has since changed. Tara Street is now the busiest station on the network and in 2005 or soon thereafter it is about to become one of the grandest. An elegant and spacious new three-storey concourse, extended platforms, restaurants and other passenger facilities will all be paid for by utilising the 'air-space' above the rail tracks.

Córas Iompair Éireann (CIE), the parent company of Irish Rail/DART, is planning to build 60m high tower over the station by utilising the real estate or air-space above the tracks, an idea likely to catch on considering the amount of valuable land over which the rail network in Dublin travels. The design of the main tower is, for a change in the Dublin context, of a curved shape, ending like some gargantuan ship's prow. Interestingly, true to its role as a public transport company, CIE has designated only a handful of car spaces in the basement (they are intended for servicing, emergency and disabled drivers only) but has provided parking for 150 bicycles. Provision has been made in the plans for the incorporation later of a metro level. The owners of Kennedy's Pub decided that their premises were going to stay and in so doing they have created a quirky but welcome contrast to their towering ultra-modern neighbour.

Under the National Development Plan, published in 1999, the government has committed huge resources to the upgrading and modernisation of public transport in Ireland. 'On Track' is a €1.3 billion investment programme by Iarnród Éireann (Irish Rail), over the next 5 years or so, to upgrade and increase the railway track network, to renovate or reconstruct stations and associated facilities, to modernise signalling and level crossings and to purchase new rolling stock. In a €117 million facelift at Heuston Station an extra four platforms have been added to the existing five. Luas Light Rail will connect Heuston with Connolly Station, the latter becoming a major transport hub.

DART Commuter has already received 58 new carriages and a further 60 are on order. This increased fleet size, the current programme to extend the length of platforms at all the commuter stations and power supply enhancements will allow by 2005 the running of 8-carriage trains. Capacity will then be boosted from the present maximum of 11,000 passengers per hour per direction to over 16,000 and frequencies will be augmented from 12 to 16 per hour northbound and southbound.

Fully integrated ticketing between the various public transport services (bus, rail, trams and the proposed metro) is a priority if we are serious about moving people away from car dependency but its introduction has for a series of reasons still not come about. It was successfully introduced many years ago into most other European cities so why not here? But then, that is another story!

A brief history of the Gaelic Athletic Association (GAA)

The modern Cumann Lúthchleas Gael (Gaelic Athletic Association or GAA), now Ireland's largest sporting and cultural organisation, was officially founded in a billiards room in Miss Hayes' Commercial Hotel in Thurles on Saturday, 1st November 1884. The initial full name of the new organisation was 'The Gaelic Athletic Association for the Preservation and Cultivation of National Pastimes'. The seven founder members were Michael Cusack, John Wyse Power, Maurice Davin, John McKay, Joseph O'Ryan, J. K. Bracken and Thomas St George McCarthy. At the beginning there was more emphasis placed on the athletics than on hurling or football.

The history of Gaelic Games goes back much further than the foundation of the GAA. A 9th century text, taken from the legendary saga 'Táin Bó Cualigne' ('The Cattle Raid of Cooley') refers to the hero Cú Chulainn taking "his hurley stick of bronze and his silver ball and he would shorten his journey with them". Hurling was considered a manifestation of Irish identity and nationalism and was censured and curtailed where possible from the period of the Elizabethan occupation onwards.

Ten days after the Thurles meeting, the first GAA fixtures were held at Macroom, near Cork. In 1885 the rules for football and hurling were first drawn up and were published nationwide in the 'United Irishman' newspaper. Hurling and football games were held in towns and villages throughout Munster and Leinster. The GAA had nationalistic undertones from the beginning and this factor alone ensured that, in the words of Cusack, "the Association swept the country like a prairie fire". The first All-Ireland Championships were organised on a country-wide basis in 1887 although only 12 of the 32 counties were represented across the two sports.

Croke Park, which had been used by the GAA when it was known as the City and Suburban Racecourse, was bought by the organisation in 1913 for £3,500 and then developed into the National Stadium. The 4 ha (10 acres) ground at Jones Road was renamed in honour of Archbishop Croke of Cashel, the association's first patron. Hill 16, the famous open terrace, was constructed from the rubble of the devastated city centre following the Rising of 1916. The first Hogan Stand, named after Michael Hogan, a Tipperary footballer and one of the victims of the Bloody Sunday attack by the Black and Tans on Croke Park in 1920 during the War of Independence, was built in 1924 (and rebuilt again in 1957-59). The Cusack Stand followed in 1937 and fifteen years later the Nally Stand was erected. After years of ad hoc redevelopment the decision was finally taken to totally rebuild Croke Park and work started in the early 1990s (see page 72).

Croke Park is also home to the high-tech GAA Museum, established in 1998 and incorporating the history of the GAA at home and abroad. Through the use of audio visuals, touchscreen computers, GAA memorabilia and lively interactives the museum examines the association's significant influence in the national life of Ireland.

Former Hogan Stand, Croke Park (next page): *One of the last matches to be played in Croke Park before the old Hogan Stand was demolished to make way for the new development.*

Hogan Stand, Croke Park *(2003)* - Next Page	
Medium:	*Line & Watercolour*
Size:	*594mm (Wide) x 364mm (High)*
Reference No:	*PR102*

The New Croke Park: *In the north-central district of the city the most dominant structure in the skyline is the rebuilt Croke Park, the national stadium for the GAA. The area is essentially residential and the rooflines are mainly at two or three storey level so Croke Park stands out as an elegant backdrop of Colosseum proportions. Costing over €140 million to construct, the new stands can accommodate 79,500 spectators in great comfort. Another reconstruction phase on the remaining northern or so-called 'railway end', yet to begin, will add thousands of additional spectator spaces. One of the three levels (the middle premium concourse), which is mainly reserved for corporate suites, includes hospitality facilities such as restaurants, bars and conference rooms. Relieving the otherwise built-up feel of the development is the Royal Canal which threads its rustic way around the southern perimeter of Croke Park.*

Croke Park (2003)	
Medium:	*Pen & Ink on Board*
Size:	*358mm (Wide) x 216mm (High)*
Reference No:	*DR018*

The Quays of Dublin

Central to the development of Dublin throughout the centuries was the city's commercial and physical relationship with the River Liffey. We have already seen that, around the area where the old Viking town originated, the river was once approximately five times wider than it is today. Over time, to achieve deeper water for ever larger trading vessels, the river was narrowed from both sides, firstly by the use of wooden revetments and then by the construction of stone quayside walls. The continuing search for deeper water drove the docklands ever further eastwards so that today Dublin Port occupies the eastern-most extremity of the city. The following is a brief description of the name origin and dating, where known, for each of Dublin's quays (spelt 'key' on the 18th century maps, from the old French word 'Kay').

Northside Quays from Heuston Station

Wolfe Tone Quay: *C. 1860s. Named after the 1798 patriot, Wolfe Tone. Formerly known as Albert Quay, from Prince Albert, consort to Queen Victoria.*

Sarsfield Quay: *1766. After the great soldier patriot, Patrick Sarsfield (1655-93). Formerly called Pembroke Quay.*

Ellis Quay: *C. 1682. From Sir William Ellis who developed this end of the north quays.*

Arran Quay: *C. 1662. Named after Charles Butler, Earl of Arran and son of James (see Ormond Quay).*

Inns Quay: *17th century. From the King's Inns of Court, now the Four Courts.*

Ormond Quay: *C. 1677. From James Butler, 1st Duke of Ormonde, Lord Lieutenant 1643-49, 1662-64 and 1677-82.*

Bachelors' Walk: *1678. Likely named after a local property owner.*

Eden Quay: *Dates from at least 1796 and named after William Eden, Chief Secretary of Ireland, 1780-82.*

Custom House Quay: *1790. Named after the new Custom House.*

North Wall Quay: *Originally built 1729. Named as such because it was built on the north bank of the river.*

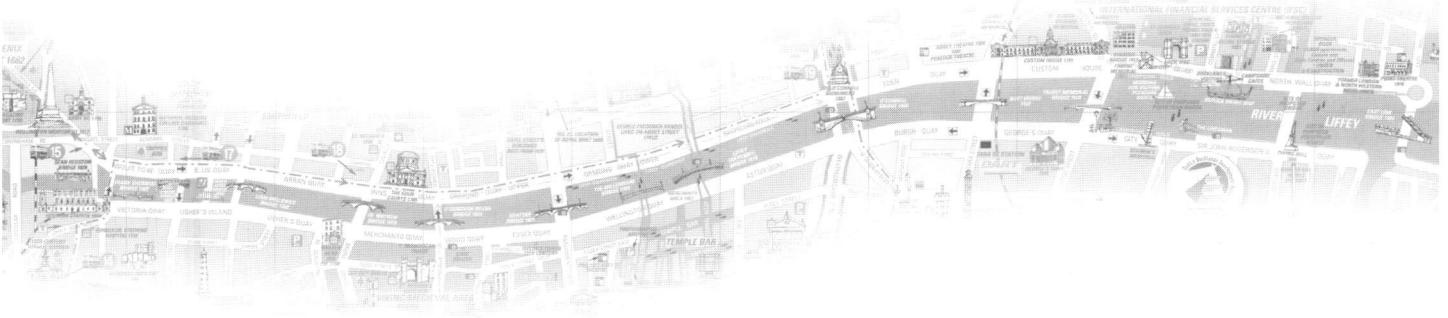

Southside Quays from Heuston Station

Victoria Quay: *C.1860s. From Queen Victoria, Queen of England 1837-1901.*

Usher's Island: *C. 1670s. Named after John Usher, Town Sheriff and Mayor, who lived here from 1557 when the site was indeed an island (see map on page 6).*

Usher's Quay: *C. 1670s. As above.*

Merchant's Quay: *C. 12th century (originally a wooden pier, later of stone and rebuilt several times). From the time when Merchants were the main users and inhabitants of this stretch of quayside.*

Wood Quay: *C. 11th century. From the days when it was made from wood. This is the site of the city's first quay. It was first built of stone around 1300.*

Essex Quay: *C. 1680s (to replace a wooden pier and slipway). From Arthur Capel, Earl of Essex, Lord Lieutenant, 1672-77.*

Wellington Quay: *C. 1812. Named to honour Dublin man, Arthur Wellesley (1769-1852), who as the Duke of Wellington defeated Napoleon at Waterloo.*

Crampton Quay: *1766. From Philip Crampton, bookseller, City Sheriff and Lord Mayor (1696-1792).*

Aston Quay: *C. 1680. Named 'Aston Quay' in 1708. Possibly from Henry Aston, prominent 18th century businessman.*

Burgh Quay: *1808. From Elizabeth Burgh, wife of Anthony Foster, Chief Baron of the Exchequer (1766-77).*

George's Quay: *C. 1700s. From George l, King of England 1714-27.*

City Quay: *1715. Built to connect Sir John Rogerson's Quay and George's Quay. It was funded by the City (Council) and named as such.*

Sir John Rogerson's Quay: *1713. Sir John took a lease of the strand to the north of Lazers Hill and commenced to reclaim it from the Liffey.*

George's Quay: *The pyramid-topped towers on George's Quay, some reaching to 13 storeys, were completed by the Cosgrave Property Group in 2001. The cluster of pyramids are an interesting addition to the skyline as most of its modern neighbours are essentially flat-topped. These towers were the final development in a long-running and sometimes controversial battle with the planning authorities and various objectors. The site was first acquired in 1973 by Irish Life who waited until the better economic climate of the 1990s before commencing the construction of the quay-side buildings on a phased basis. The proposal to erect much higher towers than those that were ultimately built was rejected by the planners and the site behind the river frontage remained empty until Cosgrave decided on a revised scheme which offered acceptable heights. Although George's Quay is on the opposite side of the Liffey to the IFSC, it has attracted many financial services companies and, de facto, has become an extension to the international centre. Cosgrave Property Group has achieved a high reputation for superior quality apartment and office developments in, and outside, Dublin. The group also developed the Radisson SAS St Helen's Hotel on Stillorgan Road.*

George's Quay (2003)

Medium:	*Line & Watercolour*
Size:	*550mm (Wide) x 430mm (High)*
Reference No:	*WC022*

Stradbrook Hall: *Stradbrook Hall, in Monkstown, is one of the many mansions built in this general area during the 19th century when it was considered fashionable for the gentry, professional and rich merchant classes to move into the genteel suburbs of south Dublin. Quite a number of these large homes disappeared under the bulldozer in the name of progress before more recent wisdom had decreed that the survivors should be preserved. A case in point is Stradbrook Hall. It has not alone been preserved but has now found a new life as an apartment complex within a new housing development built sensitively by Sorohan Builders. It was constructed around 1830 for Richard Pim, a stockbroker and a member of the famous merchant family that owned Pim's Department Store on South Great George's Street.*

Stradbrook Hall (2003)	
Medium:	Line & Watercolour
Size:	520mm (Wide) x 400mm (High)
Reference No:	WC126

Cervantes: The Instituto Cervantes, located in a restored Victorian house on Northumberland Road.

Cervantes Institute (2002)

Medium:	*Line & Watercolour*
Size:	*371mm (Wide) x 469mm (High)*
Reference No:	*WC023*

The Instituto Cervantes

Number 58 Northumberland Road started life in the 1830s as a splendid example of a large Victorian town-house on one of the leafy suburban roads leading east from the south city to the fashionable coastal resorts of Blackrock, Kingstown (Dún Laoghaire) and Killiney. By the outbreak of the Second World War the house had passed to the German Foreign Office and was used by it until the end of the war as its legation in Ireland. It had the distinction of being the only German diplomatic mission to remain in full operation in a British Commonwealth country during the war (Ireland, which had remained strictly neutral throughout the war, did not leave the Commonwealth until 1949 when the country declared itself a republic). As might be expected, not a little controversy and suspicion attached itself to the legation during the dark days of the war. The German Foreign Minister, Von Ribbentrop, did attempt to influence the IRA to engage in sabotage and armed conflict against the British forces in Northern Ireland and in Britain. To signal the imminent invasion of England and thus the initiation of IRA activities, the staff in the legation were to have placed a red flowerpot in one of the windows. No invasion ever did take place and no record exists to clarify if a red flowerpot ever did grace a window overlooking Northumberland Road.

An act which drew opprobrium from the allies on the head of the Irish Taoiseach (Prime Minister) took place on the 3rd May 1945 when Eamon de Valera called on the German Minister, Dr Hempel, to officially express the condolences of the Irish people on the death of Adolf Hitler, who had committed suicide a few days earlier. While de Valera protested that his visit was purely in accordance with strict diplomatic protocol and courtesy (he had done the same a month earlier when he called to the American Embassy on the death of Roosevelt) it must be remembered that it was made despite the revelations of the horrors of the German concentration camps. De Valera, a man punctilious in matters of state, vigorously defended his actions but it was also clear from his own admissions that he highly respected Dr Hempel. He wrote: "During the whole of the war, Dr Hempel's conduct was irreproachable. He was always friendly and invariably correct – in marked contrast with Gray". The latter was the unpopular American Ambassador to Ireland who often expressed his scorn at Ireland's neutrality. At one time, in late 1940, Ireland fully expected an invasion, not of German forces, but of the British army egged on by America. This fear was, thankfully, never realised.

Not withstanding de Valera's high regard for Hempel (the German and his wife were granted political asylum in Ireland after the war), the legation did report by radio to Berlin on what it knew of the strengths of the Irish defence forces and on shipping movements (which once led to the sinking of an American ship). The legation's radio transmitter was later confiscated. In May 1945 the legation and its contents were surrendered to Ambassador Gray as the representative of the American Occupation Forces in Germany.

The Instituto Cervantes, a Spanish cultural institution, now occupies the house. In recent years the building has been meticulously restored by its present owner, Mr Cyril Carr, and is a pertinent example of how a fine old building can be preserved in all its original glory while fulfilling a modern and relevant role.

Guinness Storehouse: *The Guinness Storehouse, completed in 1904 to house the firm's fermentation process, is one of Dublin's most remarkable industrial buildings reminiscent of the late 19th century buildings of the Chicago School. It is a massive structure rising to an equivalent height of nine storeys. Although the outer walls are of brick the structural framing is of steel. The designer was A.H. Hignett, an engineer employed by Guinness. The contractor was McLaughlin and Harvey. The Storehouse, reopened in 2000, was redeveloped to provide a new world-class visitors complex, a corporate entertainment area, state-of-the-art training facilities, a company archive, a hospitality suite and an exhibition gallery. The view from the Gravity Bar on the top of the building gives a magnificent panorama of the whole city, a view that changes with the season or with the ever-varying Dublin weather.*

Guinness Storehouse (2003)

Medium:	Line & Watercolour
Size:	550mm (Wide) x 430mm (High)
Reference No:	WC020

Rockford Manor: *This impressive house was built in a flamboyant Tudor style popular in Victorian Ireland. It was originally erected by Sir William Betham, who held the grand title of Ulster King of Arms at Dublin Castle (he was in charge of the country's genealogical service). It was bought in the 1880s by William Bruce who then had the house further embellished. Eventually, the house was purchased by the Presentation nuns who operated a girls school from here. Sorohan Builders then acquired the house and its extensive lands and built town houses and apartments around it while turning Rockford Manor itself into a number of top-class apartment suites. It is in such ways that our heritage from the past survives by taking on a new role which then ensures ongoing protection and maintenance.*

Rockford Manor (2003)

Medium:	Line & Watercolour
Size:	520mm (Wide) x 400mm (High)
Reference No:	WC127

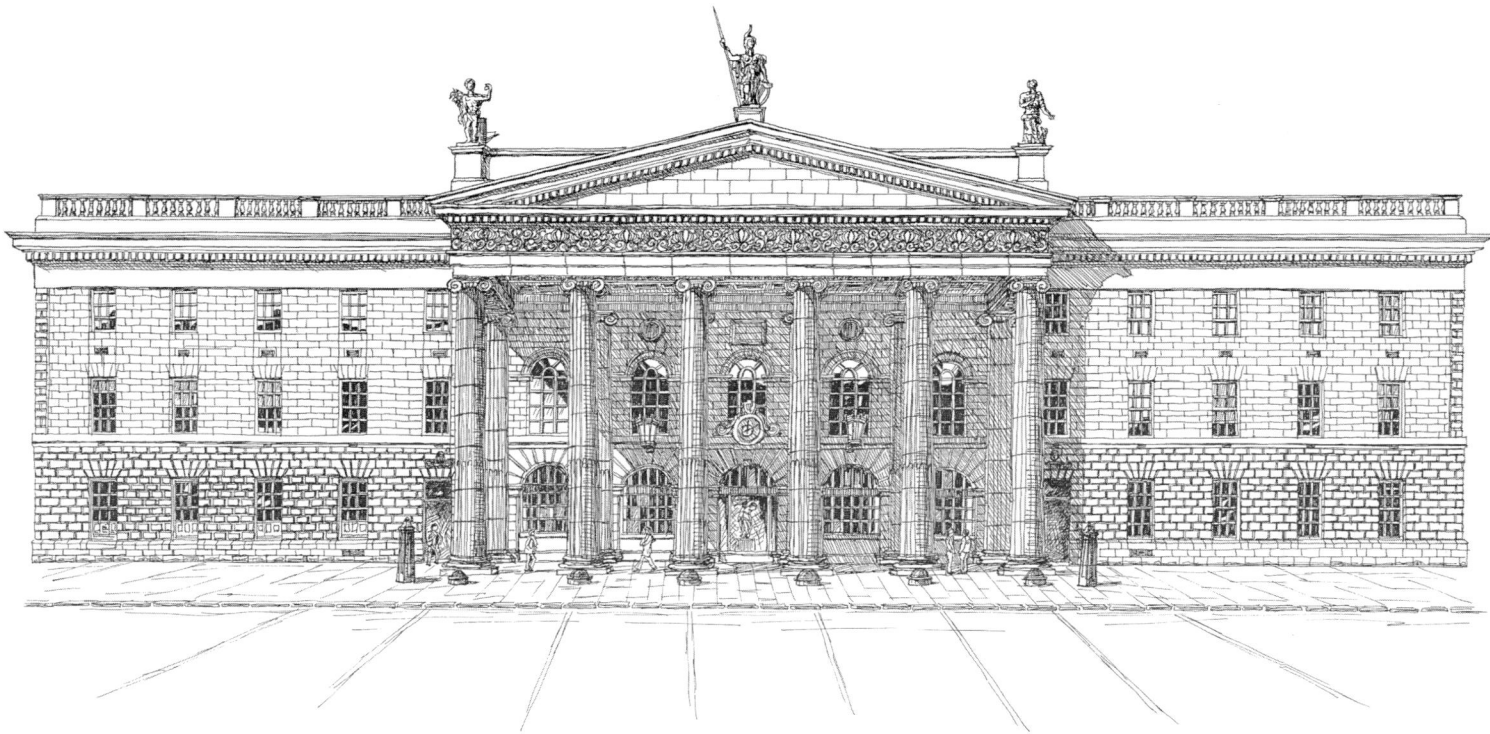

The General Post Office: *The impressive ediface of the General Post Office (GPO), on Dublin's O'Connell Street, follows the great tradition of the neo-classical architecture of Georgian Dublin. The GPO, a striking building by any comparison, was designed by Francis Johnston and cost £50,000 to build. It was opened in 1814. Granite was used throughout except for the portico and its six Ionic columns where Portland stone was employed. Surmounting the scene are Edward Smyth's sculptures of Mercury, Hibernia and Fidelity. In April 1916 the GPO was occupied as the virtual headquarters of the rebels during the 1916 Rising and was set ablaze by the British artillery. In 1929 a reconstructed GPO opened again for business. Advantage had been taken of the destruction along Henry Street to lengthen the building on that side from the original 36.5 m to 100.5 m. A further extensive renovation was carried out in 1984 to mark the creation of An Post, a semi-state company which had been formed from the old Department of Posts and Telegraphs. Inside the public office is a statue by Oliver Sheppard to Cuchulainn, a legendary Irish hero of 2,000 years ago, and a series of large oil paintings depicting the siege of the GPO in 1916.*

General Post Office (2003)	
Medium:	*Pen & Ink on Board*
Size:	*350mm (Wide) x 210mm (High)*
Reference No:	*DR104*

The National College of Ireland (NCI)

The National College of Ireland (NCI), which now has over 8,000 full and part-time students, started life in 1951 as the College of Industrial Relations and is a non-profit, third level institution committed to bringing learning into communities all over the country. NCI's student profile is somewhat unique as around 88% of its students are working adults.

In September 2002 NCI transferred its hub activities from Ranelagh to the International Financial Services Centre on a site provided by the Dublin Dockland's Development Authority where it opened its new state-of-the-art college on Mayor Street. NCI also runs over forty off-campus centres where 50% of the total student body attend courses. Distance learning, on-line courses and on-site educational centres within industry are also part of the college's structure. The college has two main schools; the School of Business and Humanities and the School of Informatics. In the new 5-storey college building there is extensive lecture accommodation as well as computer laboratories, a library with IT facilities, student residences, restaurants, a large welcoming atrium and a courtyard garden.

Fifty three apartments offering 286 separate study bedrooms are available for first year students. Other support facilities such as a student restaurant, recreation and meeting rooms, a gym and a crèche are also provided. All this will encourage and enable the students to become part of the surrounding community and to become involved locally with second-level schools in terms of mentoring and with businesses in terms of job placement and work experience. These activities will in turn link the community and business back to the college. A welcome innovation from the college is its outreach programme to the local community who are invited to use facilities such as the library, the restaurant, the Digital Learning Centre and the Community Learning Hub (rooms provided for teaching and seminars).

The arrival of the NCI into a mostly office environment not only gives the students first-hand encounters with the world of work but also infuses a collegian buzz onto the street activity and into the various local coffee shops and pubs.

Since August 2003, Excise Walk, which runs alongside the square in front of the college and to-date Dublin's newest street (but not for long!), has been the location every Wednesday for the colourful Farmers' Market, where customers can buy organic fruit and vegetables, freshly baked bread, jams and preserves, goats' cheese, fresh fruit juices and even garden plants. Such markets, relatively new to the Dublin scene, are a welcome addition to the street life. Excise Walk, which is between the Clarion Hotel and a range of apartment blocks is also a trendy pavement café street in fine weather.

NCI: *The National College of Ireland, a third-level college situated in the heart of the business district in Dublin's International Financial Services Centre. The IFSC has become more of a town within a city now that the offices and apartments have been joined by a range of educational, retail, entertainment and cultural venues.*

National College of Ireland (2003)

Medium:	*Line & Watercolour*
Size:	*530mm (Wide) x 430mm (High)*
Reference No:	*WC128*

Roches Stores: *The reconstructed Roches Stores flagship store in Henry Street, which was completed in 2003. This huge investment by the department store group underpins the resolve by the local traders to compete vigorously with suburban shopping centres.*

Roches Stores *(2003)*	
Medium:	*Line & Watercolour*
Size:	*600mm (Wide) x 420mm (High)*
Reference No:	*WC129*

Roches Stores

Roches Stores was founded in Cork in 1901 by William Roche. He started with a back lane store selling furniture for cash only (at that time the large department stores preferred credit or account customers only). William Roche, despite many setbacks, made a great success of his enterprise and in 1927 he came to Dublin to open a branch in Henry Street in the premises of the Henry Street Warehouse. This was a rather old-fashioned store but in time it was vastly improved and added to. In the 1960s, Roches Stores installed escalators, the first store in Ireland to do so. The present reconstruction, the biggest in the history of the company, reflects the importance of the location as a primary shopping precinct and is a vote of confidence in the future of Dublin City Centre. One complete floor will be given over to the giant Spanish fashion retailer, ZARA. The architects for this project, as indeed for all the Roches Stores buildings, are Newenham Mulligan Architects.

Roches Stores: *A montage of the Roches Stores premises now spread all over the country including the flagship stores in Dublin and Cork.*

chq - IFSC

In 1986, the Government established the Custom House Docks Development Authority (CHDDA) to take in hand some of the redundant dockland immediately east of the Custom House and turn it into a modern office and apartment centre. The project led to the foundation of the International Financial Services Centre (IFSC) which became the economic engine for the rehabilitation of an area eventually more vast than the original concept. Now over half the world's leading banks and insurance companies have operations here managing funds amounting to around US$300 billion. In 1997, the CHDDA was replaced with a new organisation, the Dublin Docklands Development Authority (DDDA), whose brief was extended to cover a much larger tract of land on both sides of the River Liffey. The DDDA's remit now extends to over 520 ha (1,300 acres). The 1997 Master Plan sees, over a 15 year time scale, a population increase from 17,000 to 42,000 in the Docklands region involving the construction of 11,000 new homes. Over 40,000 new jobs are expected to be created but this will depend on the continuing success of the Irish economy.

The DDDA has been a huge success story. The original IFSC was doubled in size (it now supports up to 15,000 employees across 300 domestic and international financial institutions and 3,500 residents), new high-grade pedestrian walkways (called 'campshires') have been opened along the quays of the river and one of the largest housing, office and leisure/cultural developments in the history of the state is currently underway around the Grand Canal Docks. An exciting feature of this latter scheme is Grand Canal Square, Dublin's newest public space. Built over a 150-space public car park, the square will face the waterfront and with fountains and lighting should provide a perfect setting for outdoor concerts and the like. Directly across the river is the massive Spencer Dock site, a former rail marshalling yard. Here thousands more apartments and offices will come on stream over the next few years. Spencer Dock may also see the development of a transport hub (Metro and Luas). Two new bridges, one vehicular, the other pedestrian, will link this development with Grand Canal Docks (see also pages 104, 116, 120 & 125).

One of the final projects for the original IFSC is the restoration of the old 'Stack A' warehouse which possesses one of world's earliest systems of cast-iron roof trusses. The extensive vaulted cellars are also of great interest. The warehouse was built in 1821 as a tobacco and wine store and in 1856 it was the only building in Dublin large enough to hold a banquet for the 4,000 Irish soldiers returning from the Crimean War where they had served with the British Army.

Stack A, now to be known as chq (i.e. custom house quay), will be an exciting day and night-time venue containing luxury retail outlets, trade exhibition areas, restaurants and contemporary cultural spaces. Its river frontage will be formed entirely of glass which should add a warmth and appeal to the dockside, especially at night. Some of the cultural and exhibition displays will be featured outdoors between chq and the inner St George's Dock.

The IFSC and chq will shortly be joined to the opposite river bank and the Government and cultural district around Merrion Square by a spectacular new pedestrian bridge. The winning design, unanimously selected in an international competition, was by Brian O'Halloran & Associates and will be built in association with structural engineers, O'Connor Sutton Cronin. The twin cantilevered bridge will swing on two cradles to allow shipping, mainly yachts, to pass.

chq (next page): chq (former Stack A), IFSC, is a new retail and exhibition venue in the IFSC. An additional pedestrian bridge will be built to connect it with the opposite quayside.

chq, IFSC (2003) - Next Page	
Medium:	*Line & Watercolour*
Size:	*640mm (Wide) x 420mm (High)*
Reference No:	*WC130*

The Growth of Dublin Airport

In the mid-1930s a search was on to find a suitable location for Dublin's proposed new civilian airfield. The site of a former World War One British military aerodrome at Collinstown, a convenient 8 kms from the city centre, was eventually settled upon and construction work began in 1937. A 1.6 km grass runway was laid out and construction commenced on the terminal building. In the same year the current manager of Dublin Airport, Aer Rianta, was set up by the government. The state airline, Aer Lingus (founded 1936), operated the airport's first flight in 1940 to Liverpool. By 1941 the new terminal (which still operates as a terminal) was opened. It was an impressive building designed to resemble the bridge of a luxury liner. The architect, Desmond Fitzgerald, won a major award for the design. The Second World War prevented any expansion of air services but after hostilities had ceased growth was rapid and new concrete runways were laid down. The terminal saw the glamorous comings and goings of international travellers in an era when air travel was, for the most part, reserved for the upper echelons of society, business people and for those on that scarce long-planned overseas holiday. Aer Lingus, using mainly DC3s, was the principal carrier using the airport up to 1957 when British Airways opened up regular new services. Passenger figures for 1949/50 totalled 212,661.

Operating Lockheed Super Constellation aircraft Aer Lingus began transatlantic flights in 1958 and soon the large (by the standards of the day) Boeing 707 aircraft were using the airport. Rapid expansion in facilities were put into place including the building of additional terminals, hangers and cargo depots and the installation of approach lighting and radar systems. In what turned out to be a visionary move, provision, through land purchase and zoning, was made to allow the airport room to expand over the next fifty or sixty years. By 1969/70 1,737,151 passengers travelled through Dublin.

To meet the challenge of the newly introduced wide-bodied aircraft Aer Rianta undertook the construction of a large new terminal and extra piers (designed to handle 5 million passengers a year) which were ready by 1972. Aer Lingus's expanding fleet was accommodated in enlarged hanger space. Business through the airport, having expanded year on year, then took a serious reverse on foot of international recessions and on the outbreak of the Northern Ireland troubles in the mid-1970s. Growth was sporadic and unimpressive until the late 1980s. A peak in 1979 saw 2,756,561 passengers flying through Collinstown. When Ryanair, a new and cheeky low fares airline, introduced an element of serious competition on the U.K. routes passenger figures jumped beyond all expectation. Numbers increased from 2.9 million in 1986 to 5.1 million three years later. A major new runway, featuring the latest in navigational aids and safety features, was then built and it dealt exceptionally well with the increased traffic. Delays in government approval for terminal extensions, however, meant increased frustrations for travellers and staff trying to cope in overcrowded facilities. Finally, by 1999 and over the next couple of years, new terminal space, capable of handling 20 million passengers per annum, came on line.

Will this be enough? Already, over 15 million passengers came and went in 2002 and this figure is projected to rise every year until the 20 million is reached in 2005. By 2030, 30 or 40 million a year should not be a surprise. Terminals and facilities to meet this demand must be planned now. Car parks (over 20,000 spaces) are at full capacity and more are envisaged but the real solution here lies with the urgent introduction of express main rail and light rail (Luas) access. An additional parallel runway will also need to be built and the groundwork has to be laid to accommodate the new and very heavy twin-deck super jumbos now being assembled.

Whether the government continues to allow Aer Rianta to manage Dublin Airport or not – Aer Rianta, in fairness, successfully manages by any international standard one of the fastest growing airports in the world but has occasionally been restricted by government action (or inaction) and has been wrongly blamed in the past for terminal space shortcomings – the efficiency and good health of the airport is vital for the well-being, prosperity and future of Dublin City itself.

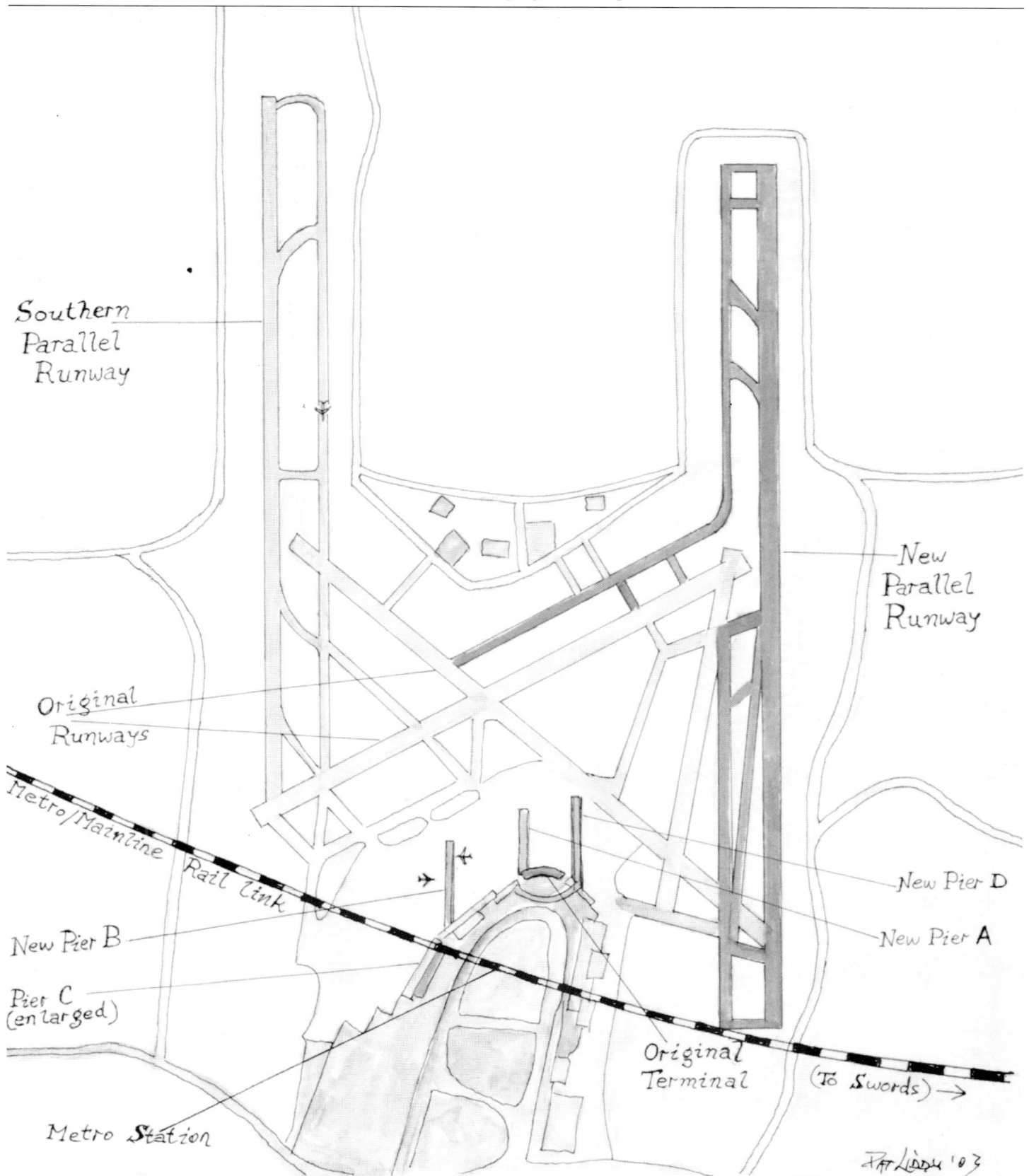

Southern
Parallel
Runway

New
Parallel
Runway

Original
Runways

Metro/Mainline Rail Link

New Pier B

Pier C
(enlarged)

New Pier D

New Pier A

Original
Terminal

(To Swords) →

Metro Station

Pat Liddy '03

Bird's Eye View of Dublin Airport: *This view shows the extent and main infrastructural details of the airport likely to have been put in place by the year 2015. The original terminal of the 1940s and the runways of the 1950s are dwarfed by the subsequent developments.*

The Growth of Dublin Airport (2003)

Medium:	Line & Watercolour
Size:	205mm (Wide) x 255mm (High)
Reference No:	WC121

Westin Hotel

If a city-centre is composed entirely of offices and business institutions it is likely to be a dead-centre at night time when the workers are gone home. In the early 1990s, when the banks who mainly occupied the block that is now the Westin Hotel on College Street/Westmoreland Street decided to sell the property, there could have been a number of options. The market of the day indicated that offices would be the most likely solution rather than apartments or retail or a mix of both. The planners turned down the initial applications, partially on the grounds that the additional heights sought were excessive. After many delays a different approach was made when Treasury Holdings, the eventual developers of the site, opted instead for a hotel. This found more favour with the planning authorities as a hotel would bring life, day and night, to the surrounding streets.

The interior requirements of a 5-star hotel, i.e. large and well designed public areas and uniformly laid out bedroom areas, required gutting almost the entire internal structures of the block. The facades of the buildings themselves and some of the interiors, especially the opulent banking hall of the former head office of the Provincial Bank, were on the preservation list and could not be demolished. In any case, these were going to be a valuable asset to the hotel when it was finished. To achieve the protection of the preserved walls and interiors they were girdled with steel frames while the rest of the site was completely emptied and the work of rebuilding got under way.

The end result is very impressive and the new and simpler infill sections fit in very well with the more decorous Victorian facades. The interior is sumptuous, not least being the Banqueting Hall, the former banking hall. The design for the 163 bedroom Westin Hotel was carried out by Henry J. Lyons and Partners and P.J. Walls were the contractors.

College Street: *An 1850 view of College Street, the future site for the Westin Hotel, is taken from Shaw's Pictorial Guide and Directory.*

Westin Hotel, College Street (previous page): *The hotel frontage is a composite of individual buildings mostly former bank premises.*

Westin Hotel *(2003)* - Previous Page	
Medium:	*Line & Watercolour*
Size:	*520mm (Wide) x 410mm (High)*
Reference No:	*WC131*

Milltown Viaduct

Luas Light Rail: Competition between the railway companies of the mid-19th century Ireland was intense and at one time the country had more railway lines for its size than any other country in the world. But this was at a time when the population was higher than it is today (before the disasters of the Great Famine) and, of course, there were no motor cars and the condition of road surfaces was appalling.

A serious decline in the fortunes of the railway companies came after the Second World War when both petrol and cars became more plentiful. Line after line was closed down until only the core networks, serving the principal cities and towns, remained. The once excellent and technologically ground-breaking tram system in Dublin was similarly wound down from the 1930s when buses were deemed to be superior and more independent, being away from fixed lines. The last tram to run in Dublin left from O'Connell Street in 1949.

Since then traffic on the roads increased year on year until gridlock forced a rethink on public transport options and the return of the tram, albeit in a different format, was decided on in the early 1990s. Two lines are initially being built for the Luas (i.e. Irish for 'speed'); from Sandford and Tallaght. Further extensions and additional lines are planned. Some of the outer areas of these routes will eventually be absorbed into the proposed metro system. Delays by successive governments in implementing the construction phase of Luas has led to increased costs, public annoyance and inconvenience and a certain scepticism about the advantages of a light rail system. It has not helped that Government also seems confused about the difference between on-road light rail and a largely underground metro system. The former is designed for convenient, speedy and comfortable travel on high frequency services along the streets of the inner city. Commuter travel linking suburbia and business centres, where huge numbers of people need to be transported quickly between work and home, is best served by a metro heavy rail system which will go underground in densely built-up areas. So metro will not replace Luas, the two go hand-in hand, as is the experience in Europe and in several American cities. In the city-centre Luas should not go underground; if necessary cars and trucks can be routed underground for short sections to relieve congestion spots and free up streets for pedestrians. If anything, several more interlinked Luas lines need to be built within the inner city core to make movement safe, convenient and predictable without the need to bring the car into town.

Forty tram units, made by Alstom S.A. in Spain, have already been delivered. Each standard 30m long tram can carry around 235 persons and at peak times there will be a tram every five minutes. Maximum speed is 70km per hour.

Milltown Viaduct *(2003)*

Medium:	*Line & Watercolour*
Size:	*530mm (Wide) x 430mm (High)*
Reference No:	*WC018*

Milltown Viaduct: *Until recently the old Milltown Viaduct stood as a lonely remnant of the once proud Dublin to Bray railway line which commenced from Dublin's Harcourt Street Station. It was inaugurated in 1848 and closed almost exactly 100 years later. The nine-arched bridge was thankfully left standing and has now been again pressed into service for the new Luas line from Sandyford to St Stephen's Green. The stonework of the bridge has been carefully restored by the Railway Procurement Agency, the body responsible for the construction of the Luas network. The RPA even rehabilitated the nearby elegant old chimney stack.*

Belgard Castle: *Belgard Castle, near Clondalkin, Co. Dublin, is the headquarters of CRH (Cement Roadstone Holdings) plc, one of Ireland's foremost companies and one of the top building materials group in the world. CRH was formed through a merger in 1970 of Cement Ltd (est. 1936) and Roadstone Ltd (est. 1949). In that year CRH had sales of €26 million (95% in Ireland). By 2001 sales had grown to €10.4 billion from over 1,500 locations in 22 countries.*

Belgard Castle and its estate were acquired by CRH in the 1960s for its huge limestone reserves. Belgard Quarry is now one of the largest integrated quarries under single ownership in Europe with aggregate production in excess of two million tonnes per annum. The castle itself was founded by the Anglo-Normans over 800 years ago as a defensive bastion on the perimeter of the Pale, the area around Dublin under English control. The tower is now the only remaining part of the medieval fortress as the rest of the house dates from the 18th century. The Talbot family (their northside relatives held Malahide Castle) lived here until the early 19th century, the castle subsequently passing through many other owners until purchased by CRH. Since then the house has been meticulously restored and the extensive grounds and parkland, which teem with wildlife, have been carefully managed.

Belgard Castle (2003)	
Medium:	*Line & Watercolour*
Size:	*315mm (Wide) x 210mm (High)*
Reference No:	*WC125*

Stephen's Green Shopping Centre

In November 1988 the Stephen's Green Shopping Centre opened as the then largest shopping centre in the country. The construction of the conservatory-styled building ended a phase of great uncertainty which had hung over the site for close on twenty years. The block facing St Stephen's Green West and King Street South had been assembled over a long period by a developer who had his own plans for its renaissance. He ran into financial difficulties and after much controversy the site passed to another owner. Meanwhile, several of the properties became vacant and fell into disrepair or were demolished. In fact, for a while one of the vacant sites housed the celebrated Dandelion Market, a very popular open-air market selling all kinds of trendy clothes and accessories and second-hand bric-a-brac. U2, the famed rock group, played some of its earliest gigs at the Dandelion Market. Holding out until the site was finally cleared for the building of the centre by Power Securities and British Land were the famous drinking emporia on King Street South; Rice's (at No.1/2) and Sinnott's (No.3). When the doors of these renowned pubs closed for the last time part of Dublin's heritage was snuffed out.

Today, the striking architecture of the centre (the architect was Jim Toomey) forms a strong focal point at the top of Grafton Street and, indeed, acts as that shopping precinct's anchor tenant, so to speak, drawing more than a quarter of a million shoppers and tourists into its bright and bustling interior every week. Along with the other main city-centre shopping complexes such as those on Henry Street, Mary Street and O'Connell Street (e.g. Arnotts, Roches Stores, Jervis Centre, Brown Thomas, Clerys etc.), the Stephen's Green Centre seeks to copper-fasten the centre of Dublin as the country's primary shopping venue. This means providing adequate car parking (the Stephen's Green Centre car park can hold over 1,000 cars), a variety of shopping experiences (over 100 at the centre), restaurants and cafés (with views over St Stephen's Green or down Grafton Street) and seasonal changes (Christmas on Grafton Street and in the centre is transformed by lighting and festive decorations).

An examination of the businesses carried out at this corner of Dublin (St Stephen's Green West) over a period in the century or so before the block was demolished, clearly illustrates how a city typically and relentlessly evolves (details taken from the Thom's Dublin Directory).

No. 135:
- *1856* - *Arthur Jones, Son & Co. Upholsterers, Undertakers, Valuators, Auctioneers and Cabinetmakers to Her Majesty's Board of Works (from the cradle to the grave, you might say!).*
- *1900* - *Still Arthur Jones in proprietorship who has now added shop and bank fitting, carpet, chintz and silk merchandising, house furnishings, timber and insurance agencies to his portfolio.*
- *1965* - *R. Strahon & Co. house and hotel furnishers, removal and storage contractors.*
- *1976* - *Vacant.*

No. 136:
- *1856* - *Charles Leet, Surgeon and Apothecary.*
- *1900* - *Herman Schreler, Ladies Tailor and mantle manufacturer.*
- *1965* - *New York Pressing Company and The Neptune Gallery.*
- *1976* - *Trash Boutique.*
- *1986* - *Demolished.*

No. 137:
- *1856* - *Vacant.*
- *1900* - *W & A Gilbey Wine Growers, Shippers, and Distillers.*
- *1965* - *Cards Galore.*
- *1976* - *Upstairs-Downstairs Boutique.*
- *1986* - *Demolished.*

No. 138:
- *1856* - *Mrs Reeves, Court Dresser.*
- *1900* - *M. Lawson, The Corset House.*
- *1965* - *The Green Gem Snackery and Thuillier's Ltd., Ladies Hairdressers.*
- *1976* - *Oriental Crafts.*
- *1986* - *Demolished.*

No. 139:
- *1856* - *Jones & Lovely, Family Mourning Warehouse.*
- *1900* - *Cycle Depot Ltd.*
- *1965* - *George Brown & Son, Chemists; Thomas Miller, Opticians and Gael Linn.*
- *1976* - *George Brown & Son, Chemists; Thomas Miller, Opticians.*
- *1986* - *Vacant.*

No. 140:
- *1856* - *N. Carberry, Boot and shoe warehouse.*
- *1900* - *Miss Alice Betts, Umbrella Manufacturer and M. Vance, Photographer.*
- *1965* - *William Ferguson & Son, Confectioner.*
- *1976* - *Vacant.*
- *1986* - *House of Cards.*

No. 141:
- *1856* - *Felix Nugent, Vintner.*
- *1900* - *Mrs Bolger, Wine and Spirit Merchant.*
- *1965* - *R. Rice, Wines and Spirits.*
- *1976* - *R Rice, Bar.*
- *1986* - *R Rice, Bar (it seems that the liquor trade is the most enduring!).*

By 1976 fourteen premises were vacant along the King Street side of the block and all except Rice's were demolished or vacant by 1986.

Stephen's Green Shopping Centre: *An interior view of the centre featuring the huge clock, the largest in these islands (larger even than the face of Westminster's Big Ben), made by Stokes Clocks & Watches of Cork. Stokes have erected nearly 400 public and antique clocks around Ireland including those fronting Easons and Clerys on Dublin's O'Connell Street.*

Stephen's Green Shopping Centre (2003)

Medium:	*Line & Watercolour*
Size:	*530mm (Wide) x 430mm (High)*
Reference No:	*WC021*

Iveagh Court: *Iveagh Court, a development finished in 2003 at the corner of Harcourt Road and Charlemont Street, was developed by Alcove Properties. Several other prestigious new buildings and refurbishments have also been completed in the immediate area. A new bridge over the nearby Grand Canal will bring the Luas light rail around the back of the Iveagh Court block before swinging onto Adelaide Road and down Harcourt Street past the former terminus for the Dublin to Bray railway line. All this is totally uplifting and putting new life and character into a part of Dublin that had quietly moldered away for decades.*

Consisting of both offices and residential apartments, Iveagh Court is a high specification development designed by the late Jimmy O'Connor of Arthur Gibney & Partners. The building is designed around a large central inner courtyard featuring landscaping and a car set-down area. On Charlemont Street Alcove Properties restored a period house and successfully integrated it into the scheme. It now serves as a company head office. Alcove also developed the huge Malahide Marina scheme from a redundant boatyard thus rejuvenating one of the city's most picturesque seaside resorts.

Iveagh Court (2003)	
Medium:	*Line & Watercolour*
Size:	*550mm (Wide) x 430mm (High)*
Reference No:	*WC028*

The Four Courts: *The Four Courts was designed by James Gandon, the same architect who was in charge of the Custom House further downriver. Thomas Cooley, architect of the Royal Exchange (now City Hall), had already built a public office on Inns Quay which Gandon proceeded to incorporate with some modifications as the West Wing, building a similar East Wing and joining the two to a central dome core with arches and arcades. The foundation stone was laid in 1786. The first court sessions took place ten years later and by 1802 the whole splendid array was completed.*

The Four Courts (2003)	
Medium:	*Pen & Ink on Board*
Size:	*290mm (Wide) x 245mm (High)*
Reference No:	*DR103*

Part 03
Old Places - New Faces

Sometimes there is no more daunting or upsetting emotion than that arising from the experience of profound change. Change, much of it quite drastic, is transforming vast areas of Dublin including districts unaffected by progress for decades before. This can disorientate people until the dust settles and they can begin to adjust to unfamiliar surroundings and perhaps rediscover that some of the old character is not lost but rather reinforced or enhanced by the new development. Buildings, structures or amenities worthy of safeguarding and preservation are now being integrated into new schemes and often form the anchor point for strengthening an area's unique identity. Of course, some places will appear not to change at all, like the Phoenix Park, but even here there has to be an active management strategy to maintain and enhance the park's integrity. The erstwhile rural landscape, especially on the less developed northside of the city, is now being intensively built on, mostly in a high-density format. But the local topographical features such as the River Tolka, the Royal Canal, the coastline, woods, parkland and historic monuments are being woven and integrated into the new schemes in a positive way unknown a generation ago. The best of these major developments will also have a central core, a village or town centre, if you like, which will create a sense of place and offer a comprehensive range of services to the residents.

The city centre too is modifying to become more of a people-place offering higher levels of entertainment, culture, shopping, relaxation and environmentally friendly surroundings. If a balanced mix of residents, including more family units, is to be encouraged to live in the city then apartments need to be larger and properly served locally by essential amenities such as shops, leisure areas, schools, medical clinics and so forth. Personal safety and law and order issues need to be addressed. Traffic needs to be reduced and in some cases virtually removed in favour of public transport and this means huge capital investment in transport infrastructure and the endurance of a great deal of inconvenience while these facilities are being put into place.

Complete districts are being reinvented; Smithfield, Inchicore, the Markets Area, Kilmainham, Blanchardstown, Clonsilla, Dundrum, Finglas, Docklands, Barrow Street, Grand Canal Quay, Kinsealy, Ballymun and Ashtown to name just some of them. What it is to be a Dubliner is being redefined with the welcome influx of residents from many overseas countries; not a new phenomenon for the city in historical terms, it must be remembered. Everywhere and everything appears to be rapidly changing into the unknown but hopefully the essentials – the individual characteristics of neighbourhoods and their denizens – will remain the same.

Magazine Fort: *'Behold the proof of Irish sense, here Irish wit is seen:*
When nothing's left that's worth defence, we build a magazine'.

These words by Jonathan Swift greeted the building of the Magazine Fort, a munitions storage compound, in 1732. It stands on St Thomas's Hill, the site originally of Phoenix House, a residence which gave its name to the whole park. The name 'Phoenix' is a corruption of Fionn Uisce, the Gaelic words for clear water, which is a reference to a well once located near Áras an Uachtaráin, the home of the Irish president. The star-shaped appearance of the fort's stout walls is easily discernible from the picture. No munitions were stored in the Magazine Fort subsequent to 1939 and perhaps some day it could be turned into a military museum.

Wellington Testimonial: *Every child who has visited the Phoenix Park remembers playing on the dizzyingly sloping steps of the Wellington Testimonial. This great monument, at 62.5 metres height, the second-highest obelisk in the world after the George Washington Monument in the USA capital, was built in 1817 to honour Dubliner, Arthur Wellesley, the Duke of Wellington (1769-1852). Only two years earlier the duke had defeated Napoleon at Waterloo. The bronze panels, depicting the military and political career of Wellington, were cast from captured cannon and erected in 1861. The three most eminent sculptors of the day, Joseph Robinson Kirk, Terence Farrell and John Hogan, each fashioned one panel.*

Magazine Fort, Phoenix Park (2003) - Opposite Page	
Medium:	*Oil on Canvas*
Size:	*885mm (Wide) x 595mm (High)*
Reference No:	*OL016*

Wellington Testimonial, Phoenix Park (2003)	
Medium:	*Oil on Canvas*
Size:	*885mm (Wide) x 595mm (High)*
Reference No:	*OL017*

Landmark Tower and U2 Studio at Britain Quay: *In an international competition for the design of a landmark tower, containing at its summit a two-floor studio for the world-famous rock band, U2, no less than 595 entries were received. The winning concept design, a twisting 60m high tower, was submitted by Burdon Dunne and Craig Henry, Architects of Blackrock, Co. Dublin. It is expected to be built by 2005/6. The light see-through appearance of the walls will be especially spectacular at night and the design is meant to reflect the solidity of the Docklands in contrast to the constant movement of the tidal ebb and flow at the confluence of the Liffey and the Dodder.*

Landmark Tower & U2 Studio (2003)

Medium:	*Line & Watercolour*
Size:	*205mm (Wide) x 255mm (High)*
Reference No:	*WC150*

Ongar

Ongar Village: In the area of Clonsilla, near Blanchardstown in west Dublin, approximately 10,000 new dwellings will be built over the next ten years or so. In the not too distant past developers tended to build row upon row of new houses which then formed into large conglomerations with very few facilities provided. Residents often had to wait for years before shops, schools and adequate public transport became available.

To give an idea of the continuing growth of Dublin take the greater Blanchardstown area as an example. In the mid-1960s only 1,650 people lived here compared to a projected 200,000 over the next few years. Rich farmland has in recent years been sold for housing developments and one such was the former Ongar Stud Farm at Hansfield, near Clonsilla, once the property of the horse-racing Aga Khan family. Manor Park Homebuilders bought this land in 1995 where they have nearly completed their development of around 2,000 homes. In keeping with the policy of containing the outward growth of Dublin this is more of a high-density development than was traditional for Dublin, where houses used to have large front and rear gardens.

In an attempt to prevent Ongar from becoming a large sprawling estate that would have lacked a central identity and provided little or nothing in the way of services, Manor Park decided to build a true village centre offering the kind of facilities normally found only in long established communities. There will be boutiques, a supermarket, general shops, specialised retail units, a restaurant and financial services as well as home-based offices, a crèche, a medical centre, townhouses, duplexes and apartments all of which will be gathered around squares and streets. Much of the parking will be discreet and off-street. In fact, it is assumed that most people living in the area will be able to walk or cycle to the village. The building style will be partly in the vernacular of the 19th century to give the centre a 'homely' feeling and a strong sense of local identity. Work on the village started in 2003 and the main street will focus in on the original old Georgian farmhouse which will be extended and turned into a restaurant.

Conscious of the history of the area, Manor Park decided to call many of the roads in the village and in the adjoining estate after the names of places and of the various owners and personalities associated down the years with Ongar and the stud farm.

Ongar: *An aerial artist's impression of the new Ongar Village where work has started to build the central 'heart' to the large housing schemes of Ongar Chase and Ongar Wood.*

Ongar Village *(2003)*	
Medium:	*Line & Watercolour*
Size:	*550mm (Wide) x 430mm (High)*
Reference No:	*WC025*

Ongar Village
Barony of Castleknock

TOWARDS BUILDING COMMUNITIES

MANOR PARK HOMEBUILDERS

The Helix, Dublin City University: *Opened in October 2002, The Helix Performing Arts Centre on the Dublin City University campus in Glasnevin, is the city's first purpose-built concert hall although it is not exclusively designed for that purpose as it can easily be converted into other uses including a conference venue or an examination hall for the college. There are three main performing spaces; the Mahony Hall (1260 seats), The Theatre (450 seats) and The Space (145 seats). The Helix was designed by A & D Wejchert Architects.*

The Helix, DCU (2003)	
Medium:	*Line & Watercolour*
Size:	*255mm (Wide) x 205mm (High)*
Reference No:	*WC122*

Dawson Street Café: *A few years ago if anyone had suggested that pavement cafés would be a feature of Dublin street life, that person would have been laughed out of court. Whether it is because of a change in climate or just a change in perception, tables outside restaurants and coffee shops are now commonplace and a delight today.*

Dawson Street Café (2003)

Medium:	*Line & Watercolour*
Size:	*255mm (Wide) x 205mm (High)*
Reference No:	*WC123*

Cow's Lane, Old City, Temple Bar: *Cow's Lane, Temple Bar's newest street (2000), occupies a central location in the 'Old City', that part of Temple Bar designated for mostly apartment living. The street is the site for an open-air continental style market every Saturday. The name 'Cow's Lane' is borrowed from a medieval street that has long since disappeared. Today, mostly high quality craft, fashion and interior design outlets front the street but pedestrian flows have so far been generally very disappointing. The former church of Ss Michael and John closes off the vista at the end of the street. This was the original site of the famous 18th century Smock Alley Theatre.*

Cow's Lane (2003)

Medium:	Line & Watercolour
Size:	255mm (Wide) x 205mm (High)
Reference No:	WC124

Dublin Port Tunnel: *This is Dublin's first major road tunnel and is currently one of the largest and most challenging civil engineering projects in Europe. It is estimated that initially around 9,000 heavy goods vehicles (HGVs) destined for Dublin Port will be taken off the already choked streets of the capital. HGVs will be allowed to travel free but cars using the tunnel will have to pay a toll. Close on two million trucks a year pass in and out of Dublin Port. Costing in the region of €625 million overall, the route of the 4.5km tunnel will connect the port directly with the M1 and M50 motorways. The twin sections of the tunnel at either end (East Wall, where the toll plaza will be situated, and the Coolock Interchange) are being constructed using a cut and cover method while the long central sections, at a depth of up to 24m, are being dug out by a massive, Japanese-built, boring machine working out from the access shaft at Collins Avenue. The tunnel, which will reduce travelling time for the 5.6km total journey from around 40 to 6 or 7 minutes, is due to be operational by 2005.*

Dublin Port Tunnel (2003)	
Medium:	*Line & Watercolour*
Size:	*255mm (Wide) x 205mm (High)*
Reference No:	*WC120*

City Hall Interior: *The wonderful interior of City Hall. The grandeur of its original classical design has been marvellously rehabilitated, if not indeed exceeded, by Dublin City Council during the restoration of the late 1990s.*

City Hall Interior (2003)

Medium:	*Line & Watercolour*
Size:	*255mm (Wide) x 205mm (High)*
Reference No:	*WC023*

City Hall (previous and next page): One of the most aesthetic of the classical buildings in Dublin must surely be City Hall. The elegant and imposing exterior is more than matched by the august majesty of the interior. An architectural competition was announced in 1768 by the Merchants' Guild of Dublin for a new Royal Exchange on Cork Hill opposite the recently opened Parliament Street. A Londoner, Thomas Cooley, won the first prize of £100 (and the commission). James Gandon, the architect of the Four Courts and the Custom House, won the second prize of £60. Construction work started in 1769 but it would take 10 years before the building was completed. The finished work was greeted with great enthusiasm and praise. In 1851 the Merchants' Guild vacated the building in favour of Dublin Corporation (now the Dublin City Council). The upstairs Coffee Room was converted into the Council Chamber (in which function it still serves) and the ground floor Rotunda was made smaller by the erection of screen walls and partitions around the ambulatory. In the late 1990s a complete refurbishment of City Hall was undertaken by Dublin City Council and the building was painstakingly restored to the original designs of Cooley. City Hall has now one of the finest Classical interiors in Dublin. In the lower ground floor is the 'Story of the Capital', a wonderful exhibition of civic life in Dublin since medieval days. There is a fascinating series of displays accompanied by historic film footage and valuable artefacts within the atmospheric caverns whose immense parabolic walls support the great rotunda upstairs. Many of the treasures on show are completely unique including the City Sword (once the war sword of Henry IV of England), the Great Mace and the 14th century City Seal.

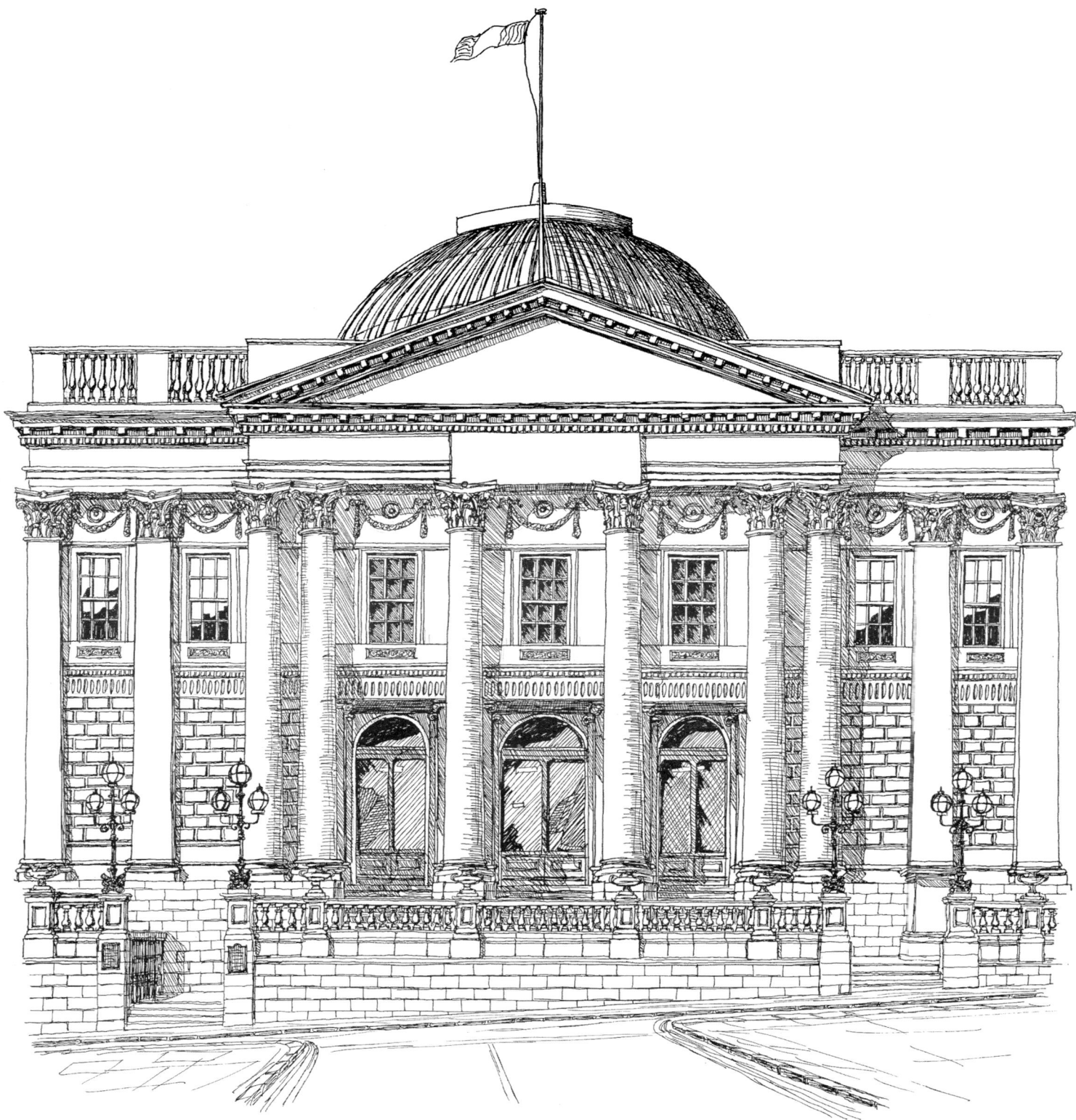

City Hall (2003)

Medium:	*Pen & Ink on Board*
Size:	*246mm (Wide) x 286mm (High)*
Reference No:	*DR020*

James Joyce Bridge: *The latest bridge to span the Liffey, named in honour of one of Dublin's literary geniuses, was designed by Spanish architect/engineer, Santiago Calatrava, and opened in June 2003. It links Usher's Island and Blackhall Place (coincidentally, no.15 Usher's Island, now being restored, was the setting for Joyce's 'The Dead') and provides an important new artery designed to relieve some of the traffic gridlock crossing the quays. As well as possessing a four-lane central roadway it also has very generous and pleasant walking platforms on both sides which allow pedestrians to better 'communicate' with the Liffey. Seats placed at the midway point encourage people to pause awhile over the river. Although small in scale compared to other international Calatrava projects it is still a dramatic structure by any standard with two splayed-out parabolic arches suspending the curving deck. It takes on a special beauty when both the superstructure and the pavements are lit at night time. Already the inspiring presence of the new bridge has uplifted what was before a rather mundane part of the city.*

James Joyce Bridge (2003)	
Medium:	*Line & Watercolour*
Size:	*255mm (Wide) x 205mm (High)*
Reference No:	*WC113*

Macken Street Bridge: *The proposed new bridge at Macken Street will carry traffic and possibly the intended extension of the Luas light rail line from Spencer Dock to the massive new docklands developments on the south side of the city. Design of the 120m -wide bridge was entrusted to Santiago Calatrava, the same architect who created the James Joyce Bridge (see previous page). It is planned that the bridge will swivel to allow the passage of tall ships and high-masted pleasure craft in and out of the city-side harbour area. Final engineering details are being worked out in this regard which may mean that the building of the bridge will be delayed until around 2005.*

Macken Street Bridge (2003)	
Medium:	*Line & Watercolour*
Size:	*255mm (Wide) x 205mm (High)*
Reference No:	*WC114*

Dublin Port: *The two chimney stacks of Poolbeg Generating Station, each 207m tall, form the backdrop to this picture of part of Dublin Port, the country's busiest harbour. High cranes, large oil facilities, shipping terminals and the world's largest car ferries are all part of the evolving skyline of Dublin Port.*

Dublin Port *(2003)*	
Medium:	*Line & Watercolour*
Size:	*205mm (Wide) x 255mm (High)*
Reference No:	*WC112*

West Link Bridge: *The original West Link Bridge, which carries the M50 over the River Liffey at the Strawberry Beds, was opened in 1989. To cater for growing traffic demands a second bridge, identical in dimensions and style to the first, was built alongside and opened in 2003.*

West Link Bridge (2003)

Medium:	*Line & Watercolour*
Size:	*205mm (Wide) x 255mm (High)*
Reference No:	*WC110*

Taney Bridge: *This spectacular suspension bridge, constructed to carry the Luas light rail line from Sandyford to St Stephen's Green, is the first of its kind to be built in Dublin. Formerly there was a stone bridge on this site but it was removed when the old Harcourt Street to Bray railway line was closed down in 1958. Subsequently, the road junction was greatly widened to facilitate the creation of a major traffic intersection. When a replacement span was called for, only a suspension bridge could then be contemplated if supporting columns spread across the roads were not to be employed. Additionally, significant traffic disruption was avoided by not having to erect temporary supports to hold up the decking of the bridge as it extended further out from the single 50m high 'A' frame. To achieve this each new length of deck was supported by connecting it immediately to the next stay in line. The 52 stays fanning out from the central pylon are designed and manufactured by VSL and contain between 19 and 37 galvanised strands. They are fixed by steel guides into massive reinforced concrete anchor blocks on the back span. The bridge, built by Graham Construction, was completed in 2003.*

Taney Bridge (2003)	
Medium:	Line & Watercolour
Size:	217mm (Wide) x 255mm (High)
Reference No:	WC111

Mayor Street, IFSC: *Almost a township in its own right, the ever-burgeoning International Financial Services Centre (IFSC) has its own main street, Mayor Street, coursing through its centre (see also page 81).*

Mayor Street, IFSC (2003)	
Medium:	Line & Watercolour
Size:	205mm (Wide) x 255mm (High)
Reference No:	WC109

Islamic Cultural Centre: In recent years the skyline of Dublin has been punctuated by more than one unfamiliar landmark. One such feature is the minaret of the Islamic Cultural Centre in Clonskea, opened in 1996. The centre ministers to the spiritual, educational and social needs of Dublin's growing Islamic community. Nor, indeed, is it kept exclusively for the use of Muslims as any visitor, just as this author experienced for himself, is made to feel welcome here. The restaurant, for example, is a popular venue for many local Dubliners. Designed by Michael Collins Associates, the building was a gift from the Al Maktoum family of Dubai.

Islamic Cultural Centre (2003)

Medium:	*Line & Watercolour*
Size:	*280mm (Wide) x 205mm (High)*
Reference No:	*WC108*

Smithfield: *Smithfield was originally an open-air market area on the west side of the inner city which had fallen on hard times. Its days when vast quantities of hay, straw, vegetables, cattle and horses were sold here were long gone by the 1980s (although there is still a horse market held here on the first Sunday of every month). The buildings around the 'square' (actually, it is a vast rectangle) had become mostly derelict and the place seemed beyond redemption. Then, the miracle happened. Under a special incentive plan managed by Dublin City Council, the adjoining old distillery of John Jameson was transformed into Smithfield Village, a complex of shops, restaurants, visitor centres, a hotel and apartments. More new buildings followed on the south and north sides and currently another large development is filling in the remaining west side. The cobbled open area has been turned into Dublin's largest civic space. The west side of this space is lined by twelve 26m-high lighting masts from the top of which are fixed gas-fuelled braziers which throw out flames to a height of two metres. The 53m-high chimney, built in 1875, was converted into a viewing platform.*

Smithfield (2003)	
Medium:	Line & Watercolour
Size:	205mm (Wide) x 255mm (High)
Reference No:	WC115

O'Connell Street: *James Larkin, a formidable trade union leader during the troubled times of the early 20th century, seems to be announcing the long-promised upgrading of Dublin's principal boulevard, O'Connell Street. The first tangible sign of the street's transformation was the erection in 2003 of 'The Spire', a 120m-tall stainless-steel clad monument designed by London-based architect, Ian Ritchie. Larkin was sculptured by Oisín Kelly in 1979.*

O'Connell Street (2003)	
Medium:	Line & Watercolour
Size:	255mm (Wide) x 300mm (High)
Reference No:	PR101

Main Street, Ballymun: *The redevelopment of Ballymun, a vast public housing complex dating from the 1960s, is probably the largest single building project to date undertaken by Dublin City Council. It involves the demolition of dozens of high-rise apartment blocks and their replacement with own-door houses. The almost €2 billion project will see the creation of a number of distinct high-density neighbourhoods served by a new main street of urban dimensions which will be lined by buildings providing comprehensive civic facilities, cultural amenities and social services as well as by private apartments, hotels and shops.*

Main Street, Ballymun (2003)

Medium:	*Line & Watercolour*
Size:	*205mm (Wide) x 255mm (High)*
Reference No:	*WC116*

Grand Canal Docks: *Opened in 1796 as Ringsend Harbour, the Grand Canal Docks had then lain more or less idle for the best part of a century. The great flour mills, which lined the inner dock, occasionally loaded ships with their products and a few abandoned boats were tied up along Charlotte Quay. All this is rapidly changing in what may become, if not the largest then one of the most significant urban projects in Dublin's history. The redundant mills are being converted into apartment blocks and the large tracts of land once associated with the manufacture of city gas are being prepared to receive offices and apartments, civic and cultural centres, restaurants and hotels. Up to 30,000 new residents will be moving into the general area including the Grand Canal Docks scheme itself, the latter being under the direction of the Dublin Dockland's Development Authority.*

Grand Canal Docks (2002)

Medium:	*Pen & Ink on Board*
Size:	*297mm (Wide) x 216mm (High)*
Reference No:	*DR102*

Gasometer, Barrow Street: *Up to relatively recently, when domestic gas was manufactured in Dublin (today, gas is piped from natural gasfields offshore), reserves were normally stored in huge containers before being distributed along the city's network of pipes. One such container off Barrow Street was supported by an elegant iron framework which has been preserved and is now being incorporated into a new apartment scheme.*

Gasometer, Barrow Street (2003)

Medium:	*Line & Watercolour*
Size:	*205mm (Wide) x 255mm (High)*
Reference No:	*WC117*

Temple Bar Dublin: *The above picture, showing an entrance into Temple Bar through Merchants' Arch, was a prototype cover for an earlier book by this author entitled 'Temple Bar Dublin'. This version was eventually not selected as the then publisher preferred to have the two maps at the top in reverse order!*

Temple Bar Dublin (1992)

Medium:	*Line & Watercolour*
Size:	*320mm (Wide) x 365mm (High)*
Reference No:	*WC037*

Temple Bar

What we now refer to as Temple Bar was originally the residential and dockland area of Dublin in the 17th and 18th centuries. The name 'Temple Bar' was then only applied to one of the narrow streets which ran, and still does, between Fleet Street and Essex Street. It was named after Sir William Temple, a prominent 17th resident of the district. When the docks moved further east the warehouses and small shops were converted into different businesses but continued to flourish. From the 1950s, however, the area went into decline as businesses, shoppers and residents moved elsewhere. From 1981, Córas Iompair Éireann (CIE), the state bus and rail company, began to purchase and assemble property bounded by Fownes Street, Dame Street, Eustace Street and Wellington Quay, with a view to building a massive Transportation Centre. While it was dealing with the planning processes, CIE rented out its properties at low, short-term rents which attracted artists, musicians and other cultural practitioners. The area took on a bohemian atmosphere and a vibrant new life began to pulsate through the streets. Residents, leaseholders and other interested people began to see a new value in the place and a committee was formed in 1988 to oppose CIE's plans. Known as the Temple Bar Development Council (the name 'Temple Bar', as referring to the whole area came out of an 1985 An Taisce [The National Trust for Ireland] report 'The Temple Bar Area – a Policy for the Future'), the committee successfully lobbied City Councillors and the Government. The then Taoiseach, Charles J. Haughey, brought his influence to bear on the matter in favour of the Development Council. CIE was persuaded to sell its land in 1991 to Temple Bar Properties (TBP), a development company set up on behalf of the Department of an Taoiseach. The remarkable regeneration of Dublin's Left Bank had begun.

Today, the process is nearly complete. The east end of Temple Bar might be more renowned for its pubs and restaurants but cultural institutions such as the Irish Film Centre, The Gaiety School of Acting, the Gallery of Photography and the Photographic Archive, a number of art galleries and studios and the ARK Children's Cultural Centre were also established. The west end of Temple Bar (west of Parliament Street) is mostly residential. It also contains some historic remains including the foundations of Isolde's Tower, the strong north-eastern tower protecting the medieval walls of Dublin, the former church of Saints Michael & John and the site off Fishamble Street where Handel's 'Messiah' had its world premiere in 1742. Cow's Lane (see page 110) is its newest street and is flanked with high quality shops. Temple Bar stretches from the River Liffey south to Dame Street and from Fishamble Street (across from the Civic Offices) east to Westmoreland Street.

Roots of the Trees 1, St Anne's Park: *Erosion from raised banks where trees were planted over the last two centuries have revealed the tortuous networks of their roots. St Anne's, now a magnificent public park, was once the estate of the famous Guinness family. The temple-like structure in the background is an attractive folly built on the crest of some high ground.*

Roots of the Trees 1, St Anne's Park *(2002)*	
Medium:	*Oil on Canvas*
Size:	*610mm (Wide) x 895mm (High)*
Reference No:	*OL011*

Roots of the Trees 2, St Anne's Park: *Another of the fantastic-shaped tree root systems in St Anne's Park, Clontarf. The classical entrance façade in the background is part of the old boat shed beside one of the park's lakes.*

Roots of the Trees 2, St Anne's Park *(2002)*	
Medium:	*Oil on Canvas*
Size:	*610mm (Wide) x 895mm (High)*
Reference No:	*OL012*

St. Colmcille's Well (2000)

Medium:	Line & Watercolour
Size:	182mm (Wide) x 194mm (High)
Reference No:	WC031

St. Colmcille's Well: *This crypt-like entrance in the village of Swords leads to where once stood a water pump and marks the original spot of the holy well of St Colmcille who was one of the early Irish church's great monastic saints. The Irish name for Swords is 'Sórd Cholaim Chille' or 'The Pure Water of Colmcille'.*

Saint Fintan's (2000)

Medium:	Line & Watercolour
Size:	182mm (Wide) x 195mm (High)
Reference No:	WC035

Saint Fintan's: *An ancient graveyard in Sutton, Co. Dublin, contains the ruins of the 9th century church of St Fintan, the patron saint of Howth. Generally, there is now a much greater awareness of the value of protecting monuments from the past.*

Cavendish Row Fountain (1998)

Medium:	Line & Watercolour
Size:	157mm (Wide) x 125mm (High)
Reference No:	WC034

Cavendish Row Fountain: One of the many decorative freshwater street fountains erected in the 18th and 19th centuries along the city's streets for the use of horses and people alike. Animals drank from the street side, humans filled their buckets from the pavement side. This fountain is located a few metres south of the Gate Theatre on Cavendish Row, on the east side of Parnell Square.

Herculanean House St. Anne's Park (2000)

Medium:	Line & Watercolour
Size:	182mm (Wide) x 195mm (High)
Reference No:	WC032

Herculanean House St. Anne's Park: Most of the follies constructed for the Guinness family when they lived at St Anne's in Clontarf (see also pages 129/130) still stand. Several were erected along the winding and tree-shaded course of the Naniken River and include this copy of a Roman house found at Herculaneum near Pompeii.

Dalkey (Cats Ladder): *Once exploited for its granite in the building of Dún Laoghaire Harbour (1817 - 1820), the defunct quarries have now found a new use - its sheer rock faces are used by practising climbers. The steps from the Vico Road up towards the top of the hill, all 238 of them, seem to go on forever when one is climbing them, hence the symbolic reference in the painting.*

Dalkey (Cats Ladder) *(1998)*	
Medium:	*Oil on Canvas*
Size:	*600mm (Wide) x 900mm (High)*
Reference No:	*OL015*

Killiney Hill: *The rich tapestry of Dublin's natural heritage is especially evident along the coastal strip or high up in the hills. One of the most breathtaking panoramas of the city and its setting between sea and mountains can be had from the top of Killiney Hill. Places like this, and thankfully the city is still blessed with many areas of rich beauty, are sacrosanct and must be kept so from pervading development no matter how forceful the pressure for building space becomes.*

Killiney Hill (1998)

Medium:	Oil on Canvas
Size:	600mm (Wide) x 900mm (High)
Reference No:	OL014

Old Man: *This proud old man, whom the artist often observed during the late 1970s, used to walk purposefully up Grafton Street until he reached the top whereupon he whipped around to stride back down again to where he had started from. He was part of the street yet not part of it. He took no notice of anyone and was ignored in return. Even then, change was happening or about to happen all around him. Four years after this picture was painted Grafton Street was pedestrianised and soon after he no longer tramped his customary way. Perhaps he didn't like the new order and moved on. Something is always lost with any change but within change it can be sometimes essential to retain and strengthen and make relevant the familiar. We need to also care more deeply that whatever the future brings every effort is made to accommodate the well-being of everybody especially the more vulnerable in society.*

Old Man (1982)	
Medium:	*Oil on Canvas*
Size:	*440mm (Wide) x 545mm (High)*
Reference No:	*OL013*

Abridged Index